Mr Newton. The man in the hat. The man that somehow makes you feel better just by being in a room with him. Paul amazes me with his talent every time I see him. If you can be one thing in life, #BeMorePaul xx

Pippa Hodge, MD of 4N Online

Paul Newton is not only an amazing magician, but the way in which he applied his unique set of skills to the uncovering of scams and security threats to individuals and businesses is extraordinary. If you have concerns about fraud, identity theft or cyber security, you NEED to read this book!

Sam Pearce, Swatt Books

I've given up trying to work out how he does it but never cease to be amazed that he can.

Simon Clarke, Radio DJ

So where do I start?!?! Been a fan for a few years now but have to say the recent mental theft "stuff" is off the scale!! This man today took passwords and PIN numbers off me...! I have no way of knowing how. Seriously amazing and very talented. Actually, scarily good! This man needs to be hired for stage shows and improving business (and personal) cyber security!!

Michael Clitheroe, General Manager of Balmer Lawn Hotel

I have performed with Paul on many a function. The reactions he gets when he steals people's personal info is brilliant. It's the one thing people remember for ages.

Matt Stirling, Magician, Mind Reader, hypnotist, stunt man, BGT finalist and he's even been in the Star Wars franchise!!!!

No matter how good I am at stealing your phone, Paul is able to unlock them and access your data by knowing your secrets!

Paul's ability to steal your personal data, passwords and more, is second to none... I may have Paul's watch, but he now seems to own my house, car and pet Labrador.

I don't trust this man but my wife thinks he's adorable... you decide who's right!

James Brown, Professional Opportunist

PIN numbers and Passwords. Neither are safe, in a room full of people watching he had them away. You SERIOUSLY need to listen to this guy. Entertaining, energetic and educational in equal measure!

Brad Burton

John!
You ARE POSSIBLY ONE
OF THE BEST HUMAN BEINGS
EVER!

THANK YOU SO MUCH FOR
YOUR SUPPORT OF ME AND
THE MENTALTHEFT MOVEMENT!
LOVE YOU!

Paul

Cover image by: JLawrence Photography
Book design by: JLawrence Photography

Printed in the United Kingdom

First Printing, 2020

ISBN: 978-1-8382541-0-0 (Paperback)
ISBN: 978-1-8382541-1-7 (eBook)

MentalTheft Publishing

MentalTheft, c/o Forest Edge Solicitors,
Suite A, Unit 1 Austin Park,
Hampshire,
United Kingdom,
BH24 3FG

www.mentaltheft.co.uk

Contents

Foreword

Hello, my name is Paul Newton, I'm a magician, a mind reader, a hypnotist and a thief. I steal information from your head all in the name of entertainment.

I've been doing this as my main income for over 10 years. Sometimes I help my brother with his business, but that's more because we have fun and spend the day together working.

I love what I do for a living and my company MentalTheft was born quite recently when I realised the importance of what my skills can actually do. I mean, just think about it, if I could use my mind reading skills to get your username and your password to your company's computers, then what else could I be doing while you have absolutely no idea that I'm there!

I could steal your bank details and log in information. And how often do you really check your bank?

I've been delivering talks on this around the UK for a while now and while I'm at these talks, I steal sensitive information from the audience.

My talk is titled "I can steal your sh1t" where I tell people exactly what I'm going to do and I still get away with it! I'm going to let you in to a little secret, people who have been to my shows know this but I'm not sure if they've told anyone. Mind reading isn't real!!!

I know. It's a shocker. But you'll get over it. I'll help you get over it if I can but I'm sure you'll pull through. Mind reading uses ancient techniques AND some things that are very new, to steal information away from you without you ever knowing what we're doing.

We use sleight of hand, trickery, magic tricks, psychology, body language, showmanship, conditioning, technology, patter, eye contact, direction, confidence, conformity, assumption, persuasion and blatant balls of steel to get what we want. We use all of these things to give you a show you will never forget.

So that's me! This book will have some scams in it, some of my thoughts around them and some very simple ways to stop YOU becoming a victim. From one talk I did a little while ago for a networking company in the UK (4Networking) we found approximately £15,000 worth of fraud that had gone undetected.

I truly hope you never go through the horrendous feeling of being scammed by a con artist.

Good luck to you, I love you all, thanks for reading!

Paulie.

Thank You To Our Sponsors

Before we get started, we want to say a massive thank you to our sponsors – people who believed in me and this project, without whom this book would never have happened. Don't forget to check out our sponsor profiles at the back of the book!

Corporate Sponsors

Aerice	Family Wise	Forest Edge Solicitors
Biscoes Law	Step By Step Listening	
Genio Accountants	Fresh Security	

Individual Sponsors

Samantha Harding	Mike Boss	Terry Murphy
Charlotte Cooper	Andy Dobson	Richie Poulton
Cathy Howells	Thomas Runacres	Matthew Ruddle
Rick Notley	Colin Bielckus	Kath Parrington-Hough
Pippa Hodge	Karen Williams	Chris Bond
Suzii Fido	Ian Dickson	Linda Bond
Alan Price	Tom Andrews	Nicky Booton
Greg Davies	Dave Lister	Shirley Moreman
Annika Wood	Kerry Anne Orr	Maddy Alexander-Grout
Robert Brown	Andrew Bunt	Matthew Parker
Kate Bickford	Alex Foden	Jason Hart
Caroline Bramwell	Keith Blakemore-Noble	Sheryl Andrews
Diane & Peter Moore	Jon Doolin	Kirsty Gray
Gavin Meikle	Ian Stapleton	Jeremy Robbins
Dominic Fenton	Andrea Hares	Alison Lee
Clive Loseby	Dan Harrison	Stuart Owers
Paul Crumpler	Jennifer Todd	Dev Sharma

Thank You!

Acknowledgements

From Paul

With love to my family, especially Kat and Emily for putting up with all of my nonsense, through writing the book, and everything else!

To my Dad, Mum, Brother, Aunts, Uncles, Nieces, Nephews, Great Nieces and Great Nephews. Thank you for being you, and helping make me the me I'm proud of.

To Mum. I wish you were still here. Your little boy wrote a book. Xxxxx

To Jesse, you have no idea how much you've helped me, not just with this book, but with so many things. You sir are an absolute diamond.

To some of my friends who helped so much that we cannot thank them enough. Samantha Pearce of Swatt Books – you are amazing! And to Keith Blakemore-Noble your kicks up my backside have been noticed.

From Jesse

To Jen, I told you we were being productive! Lots of love to everyone who was involved with this, but mostly to Jen for not hiding my body in the New Forest! Finally, thanks to Paul for being so annoying, you have literally turned being annoying into a career for us both!

Love also to our furry friends, Sammy and Luna

Chapter 1
Violation

Violated. Fear. Disappointment. Foolish. Annoyed. Angry. Weak. Depression. Anguish. Helplessness.

There are a lot of emotions that are involved when you find out that you are the victim of a crime like theft, a scam or cybercrime. Irrespective of the value, the realisation that you were vulnerable to attack.

However, there is an emotion that is more dangerous than any other, and it is one that we see from people both before and after they become a victim:

Denial

The problem with human nature is that we don't like to think that we are wrong, and we do not like to be told that we are weak. I have heard variations of the following many times:

"I have never been scammed. I did, however, find a load of direct debits coming out of my account that I had no idea what they were and had to cancel them."

How many times have you been conned, or even robbed, and dismissed it? I dare you to even contemplate the idea. The psychology that runs through people is something very important to a magician, including with mind reading. Here is the thing with magic, and the responses I get to this statement really proves my point:

"Magic isn't really magic, it's all just a trick"

The reactions I get to this are as follows:
> a. Obviously, you don't think you can fool me with that do you?
> b. I kind of realise that, but I like the illusion.
> c. Of course, it's not "really" magic. But it is though isn't it?!

Let's look at these categories, because in reality, this is how MentalTheft came to exist.

The "a" category & the birth of MentalTheft

These are the people I tend to pick on at events, the know-it-all's, the ones who say, "I can't be beaten by you". These are the people I like to steal details from, from PIN numbers to passwords! I like to mess around with them as much as possible, in front of everyone. It just amuses me.

But it is not just for the amusement, these people are normally so cocky and full of themselves it actually makes it a lot easier to trick them and break them down. If you are feeling confident that I can't steal your information in a few minutes and have made it this far into the book, you really need to read on, because you are often my first target.

The "a" category and my mischievous behaviour is where the idea of MentalTheft started to manifest itself. If you think you are strong of mind, how strong of mind do you think those are in the military? Trained to withstand interrogation, years of command experience, intelligent, experienced, feared. It was at an undisclosed military base at an evening soiree that I started a gig, just like any other.

> *"Good evening ladies and gentlemen, I'm Paul Newton. I'm a magician, a mind reader and a hypnotist, I mess with heads for a living."*

That is how I often introduce myself and tonight is no different. Tonight, I'm in a military base in the UK about to start doing some magic for a group of six people. three men and three ladies. All of them look absolutely stunning, this is a very nicely turned-out event!

I do some close-up stuff, some elastic band magic followed by a simple card trick or two. One of the officers is a bit cocky, and clearly doesn't like me being centre of attention. He starts giving me a bit of "banter".

So, I start doing some mind reading.

A few tricks in one of the guys says to me, "That's impressive but I bet you don't know my pin number" I reply "To your phone? Or your credit card?"

He looks a bit bewildered so I follow up with - "I tell you what, we'll go for your phone shall we? Can I just take your phone for a minute?"

He hands me his phone, it's an iPhone, with a 4-digit PIN that keeps it locked. I look at it for a few seconds. I look at him. I tap in 4 numbers and hand him his unlocked phone.

This is when the swearing starts.

Along with things like, "That's just not possible!"

They're a lovely group but I really need to move on. There's roughly 300 people here tonight and I need to amaze as many of them as possible.

As I'm saying my thank yous and good-byes to this group one of them pulls me to one side and has a very serious look on his face.

"Was that real?" He asks.

"Well put it this way, I went through security, so could anyone else have sneaked in with me?"

"No, this is a very secure site." He confirms.

"And do you think that any of the people on this base would have willingly given me that private information about you?"

"No, they have my back, I would trust them with my life. And most of that information is not exactly available." He says, looking increasingly stressed.

"So, the only way I could get that information from you is because I have directly taken it from you."

"Oh."

At this point I am feeling fairly pleased with myself – like I have said, I like causing a bit of fear and surprise in people like this. After a few moments of silence, he says something that changed my view on the world completely.

> *"Paul, have you thought about the security implications your skills could have on most of the organisations in this country? Maybe even in the world?"*

I've delivered training to companies in the UK in the past, teaching how to use psychometrics to better manage people in the workplace, but I had never thought about helping companies with security.

But think about this. Many companies spend a fortune on making their computer networks hack proof. But what if the hacker didn't need to hack the technology? What if they just hack the brains of the workforce? Through the years, the work I have done alongside a lot of IT experts, one of which I am not, has shown that it's a very well-known fact that people are the weakest link in security. So, what does it mean if I can hack into people's minds?

Direct access, to everything in your network. And you won't even know we're there.

The MentalTheft idea was born.

The "b" category

People who don't mind the illusion. Most people go through a stage of "I now know that Santa doesn't really exist, but I like the illusion and besides, I get something out of it." This way of thinking is just human nature – psychologists and sociologists have known for a long time that the idea of lies and "liking" being lied to is part of human nature. Whether it's the endorphins from being told we look younger than we are, to free money from the tooth fairy, or simply just keeping the peace in social circles, lies are a part of our society.

The problem is, accepting this is subconscious. When someone exploits it, we don't even see it happening – even if we are told! That's the bit that baffles people the most about my stage show - I tell you I am going to steal from you before I do it!

The reality is that most people are in the b category. You are the people most likely to read this book (fully), and you are the ones that are likely to take on board the information and get the most out of it. You are intelligent and open minded. In reality, having awareness and acting on it is the most important thing that you can do, and being in the b category means you are the most likely to do that.

Side note – I know that Santa and the tooth fairy are 100% real ok? I'm just using them as an example and if anyone of a younger age reads this please remember that you have to end up on the good list for Santa to come and visit! Everyone happy now? Oh my word that could have caused some issues!

The "c" category

There is a big part of society that likes to believe in things like magic, conspiracy theories, etc, etc, etc. Scientific study has shown that there are certain mental states that mean that certain people will believe in these things, and other people won't. It is essentially pointless having an argument about who is right and who is wrong, because neither person can (or at least is willing) to change the way their mind works. The c category is often hit and miss with taking on board what I have to say for a range of reasons, but mostly because I say that things are tricks and not magic!

But I want to help as many people as possible, so let me say this. With the above in mind, the way that you apply logic to situations is different to type b people. And it is typically a type b mindset that breaks in and steals stuff from you. This is very dangerous for the type c, because you might cause you to disregard what I am writing – which puts you at a very high level of risk. I urge you to read on, and even if you do not agree, take on board that this is how things are done and this is how you should protect yourself.

An understanding of people

As you can see, understanding who you are and what your weaknesses are is a big part of what this book is about. I have spent years fooling people as a magician, but I have also had a career in helping the staff in companies work together better through understanding personality types.

You will see on the front cover, or in most of the work I do come to that, a name that floats around quite a bit! That name is Jesse Lawrence, a man I befriended because he makes me look pretty in pictures (he is a wedding and events photographer) and because he is a really nice guy. As a marketing manager for an IT company, it turns out that he is also quite a technical person, which means his skill set in understanding tech and understanding the way that people think has made him an invaluable asset to MentalTheft.

Throughout the book you will see some of Jesse's comments and thoughts, so I thought I had better introduce him! I am, of course, aware that he may edit parts of the book that I forget to check – so I had better be nice to him!

A book for everyone

As the idea of MentalTheft grew, I became a prominent speaker for events, from networking to large corporate events, to business seminars. I get paid a lot of money by spreading awareness in businesses and giving guidance on how to make every individual more secure. But the thing that really struck me with this is that a lot of the immediate reaction I get is from people who notice scams in their private life. This really does affect everyone.

I wanted to write the book for those unable to come to an event, or who can't afford to have a professional speaker. Because every scam that we stop from happening is a win for the whole of society.

Don't worry, you don't have to become a computer whizz or a nervous wreck. Scammers are lazy and will go for the easiest target. You have probably heard the famous story/joke of the hikers and the bear, but it is very representative of the point that I am making so I am going to tell it anyway!

> *Two hikers were walking through the woods. All of a sudden, they see a bear, and the bear sees them. Looking rather annoyed that they are in the bear's territory, it starts to make its way over. One hiker hurriedly takes off his boots and puts on some comfortable trainers.*
>
> *The other hiker says, "There is no way you can out-run that bear."*
>
> *"I don't have to," he says, tying up his laces, "I only have to out-run you."*

This will hopefully make the point – but if you don't get it, here is what it is. Not everyone can afford Ministry of Defence level of security - it is just not that practical, and frankly it's still not impregnable. There is no such thing as a completely secure system, but making an effort is better than not making an effort. The more you do, the better your chances; just like a lion hunting wildebeest, scammers and thieves always go for the weakest targets first.

Chapter 2
The Three Types of Mental Theft

MentalTheft as a brand name has become well known, but what exactly is Mental Theft? Whether it is using magic, or just down right mischief, you will see that most scams fall under the guise of one of three types of Mental Theft:

The Steal
Placement
Belief

These may sound obvious; they may sound a bit cryptic. I am going to go through the different types of Mental Theft, with some interesting examples. If you can understand what criminals are trying to achieve, then hopefully you will be able to protect yourself against scams you haven't heard of yet. Of course, it means I need to be even more cunning with my magic shows!

The Steal

The steal is almost obvious – this is where someone takes something from you. This can be anything from pickpockets, breaking and entering, or even stealing data from your business.

This is by far my favourite type of theft. And I say that carefully. Because I fully understand that anyone who has had anything stolen from them goes through a whole range of emotions. I'll explain it from the point of view of an entertainer.

If I want to steal your watch, or your wallet, or even your tie, I need to distract you. I need to gain your confidence and I need to create a reason for you to look the other way. This can be seen almost as a dance and the thief is the lead dancer.

I walk up to you and express an interest in your suit jacket. I remark on how nice the material is and engage with you on the quality of the lining. While doing this I am figuring out what type of watch you have, where your keys are, where your phone is and where your wallet is.

If I have done this well then you will allow me to open your jacket again to admire the lining of the other side of the jacket, while looking at it with me I'm using my free hand to lift your wallet or phone from your inside pocket.

If done well it can truly be amazing. From evaluation of the mark to a complete steal that the mark hasn't even noticed in a matter of seconds.

If you ever get a chance to see the magician James Brown do a stage pickpocket routine, please do watch it! He is the man who taught me the beauty of how pickpockets work – he also taught me how to undo someone's watch from their wrist without them ever noticing!

A steal can be as simple as the pickpocket taking your purse while you're on public transport, maybe they took the whole purse while it was under your chair at the cinema? They could have taken your phone in the few seconds that you left it on top of a counter while you were paying a bill.

However, it was done, the steal can leave nasty emotional scars for years to come. The moment of realising something has gone, to double checking and triple checking that it has in fact been stolen, to the realisation that you may have to cancel all of your credit cards and maybe even get new keys cut to your house. Any kind of steal can have a massive effect on a person and/or a business.

Placement

When I talk about placement, I normally hear people in the audience start mouthing the word *Inception* to one another. After the film, everyone seems to be familiar with the idea. However, no-one really believes in a machine that lets us go into levels of people's dreams to create an inception idea, so it gets dismissed. But Inception, or placement as a scammer would call it, is real and is extremely dangerous.

Sometimes I may not be trying to steal something physical, but I am after data of some sort. This is where the placement of an object, a program or even a bit of technology can be the best form of deception. This can cause damage to a person and a business in so many ways.

For example – placing a keylogger onto your home computer would mean it would tell me every single keystroke you ever make on that machine. Placing an audio listening device into the office of the CEO could give me massive information about their company and any deals going on. Placing a small Pi computer into a server room could give me access to your whole company's computer network.

I use the placement method a lot when I get asked to check a company's security systems. Most companies make sure their firewall is the best possible and that their email server is as hack proof as it can be. But I hardly ever go in via the internet.

I will pretty much ALWAYS make a physical entrance onto a client's property, then I will connect the piece of kit that one of my tech geniuses has told me to plug in (I'm so untechnical that I hardly ever know what they're even called) but it gives my team remote access to whatever they want it for. If you think it's not possible, ask yourself this – have you ALWAYS stopped EVERY person that you didn't recognise when you're at your place of work? The guy with the clipboard or the delivery driver who was given access to floor 8 to make his delivery? That could have been me.

Once someone has access, either by putting an idea in your head, or an access to your system, it can be very difficult to even spot that someone is stealing from you. It's even harder to stop them. This is the idea behind ransomware – a hacker gains access to your system, and takes their time working out how to lock you out. It is likely that you will have to pay to gain access, and how sure are you that they have really gone?

Belief

Mark Twain said:

> "It ain't what you don't know that gets you into trouble. It's what you know for sure that just ain't so."

The belief element of Mental Theft is making you believe something is true when it isn't. Phishing emails, dressing up as a security guard, scam phone calls – belief is one of the biggest parts of modern scamming, and you will see it all the way through this book.

Belief is one of the mostly closely guarded things that any human being can hold onto. If you're a religious person then no one should attack your firmly held beliefs on that subject. If you're an avid follower of a specific football team then why would anyone ever try to tell you that their team is better? And what about authority figures? If you believe that a person of a certain rank or job title holds some form of authority over you than who am I to question that belief?

I'll use it, but I won't question it. This all sounds very clever – but how does all of this come together?

If I can make you believe I have a position of authority which would give me access to your company's building, why would you stop me? I could be the security guard with full ID and a phone number that you can call to verify who I am. I could be the

Fire Safety officer who needs to do a quick routine check of all of the fire doors and fire extinguishers within your office. Saying no to someone like that COULD lead to fines and possible closure of your workplace! And he has the right paperwork... And he's got the ID... He has the right logo on his polo shirt...

This belief is becoming ever more prevalent in scams, as you will see throughout this book.

3 in 1

Any one of these three types of Mental Theft are powerful and scary on their own. But a good scam artist will use all three, separately and together. It's a scary thought, but at least we know what we are up against!

Chapter 3
Your Home "Computer"

If we were to go back only around ten to fifteen years ago, the under thirties were running the world of technology – it was starting to be taught in schools, it was coming into the work place and the younger generation were finding it easier to adapt. Since the iPhone was first launched in 2007 (I bet some of you feel really old now, and will be checking that on your smart phone!), things started to change, with computers being user focussed and thus easier to be used. Fast-forward to 2020 and we have everyone using smart devices, from 6-month-old babies to great grandparents.

This is great, technology is fantastic, and businesses are relying increasingly on this tech. But now, computers are less the complex machine that you need to understand the workings of and more something that you just need to be able to use, which means that scammers can connect with every one of us in our own homes. There is more cybercrime than there are people to police it, which means that the onus is on us to protect ourselves, our friends and our families.

Passwords

One thing I talk about a lot is passwords. People think that because you have a password that everything is impenetrable; let me tell you now that it isn't. With that in mind, if I can guess your password or the pin number to your phone, what level of access do I have to your bank accounts, spending your money, taking your data? If I read through the documents on your computer or in your cloud storage, can I work out how to access more of your online accounts?

My last phone, like many phones, needed a four-digit pin number to open it and if somebody opens that phone they can get into my notes, my emails, essentially my whole life! Basically, I'm screwed!

Most phones out there now have the technology to be locked down to biometrics. For example, my daughter's phone uses her face and facial recognition as the only way to unlock her phone, whereas I use a fingerprint for my phone. This stuff is genius; we have the technology to make stealing our stuff so much harder for the fraudsters but for some reason people are sticking with the four-digit pin. This is often down to not understanding the technology – people are worried that businesses have our biometrics stored and that we are giving away certain freedoms.

The reality is that there are things in place that mean that your personal information, such as your face or fingerprint, are not accessible to anyone. IT People call this tokenization, which means that the risk to you of someone doing something with your fingerprint data is infinitesimally small compared to what they could do by just logging in to your phone with your pin number.

Jesse's explanation on Tokenization

If you are not IT literate, it is very difficult to understand what tokenization really is. In basic terms, this means that something that is stored by a computer is replaced by a code that can't be broken, as it is randomly generated and has no relation to your original data. It means that even if someone breaks encryption, it is practically impossible to steal that information.

Even laptops now have fingerprint scanners and facial recognition, but unfortunately if something goes wrong, we still revert to simple pin numbers for access. This is largely due to the reliability of the technology, but as this is becoming the norm, there is no need for us to add a weakness into the security.

As users of the tech, we need to embrace things like two factor authentications, the fingerprint technology and the facial recognition software. Not only does it keep our information more secure on our own machines, but it also means our machines are less valuable to thieves. Think about it; if you've got a lovely shiny phone but they can't even turn it on, what's the point of stealing in the first place?

Key logging. Yeah, this one is a bit nasty and a bit weird at the same time but did you know that these programs can be installed on your computer? They will log every single key ever pushed on the laptop or on the computer so just think about it for a second.

This is typical if you're in a relationship where there is no trust or if you're in a workplace where people are trying to steal your information. If you log into Facebook on a machine where a person who has that key logging software installed, they will likely have your username and your password!

Think about it a bit further and it gets scarier. If you log into your bank, if you log into your emails, if you login to your credit cards, from any machine that has a keylogger on it, I've got your access.

Again, this is something that we can beat if we use two factor authentication or even fingerprint technology!

Don't make it easy for them!

But remember, locking your machine or phone is not the only place where we have a password. Our social media, our Apple and Google accounts, our emails, our banks, our work, etc, etc, etc. Everything these days has one or many passwords. In reality, pretty much every person who reads this book knows deep down that they don't use different, highly complex passwords for every account. They certainly don't update them regularly. And if you do, you are probably not remembering them, which worries me greatly that you are storing them in some other insecure way, such has having them all saved on a document on your computer, or written on sticky notes attached to your computer.

You will notice the layers in that last paragraph – that is because when I start talking about passwords, we all know what we should be doing, and we all know that we are doing it wrong to some degree, basically because its more than we, as human beings, can be bothered to do. Which puts everyone at risk!

To help me out, I brought along a friend who I have been through all of this with before! Because it is easy for me to bleat on about what you should do but hearing it from a muggle might really help!

Please welcome on stage left (did I mention I used to work in theatre?!) the wonderful Sheryl Ann Andrews, author of *Manage Your Critic* – turn overwhelm into clarity in 7 steps. See? Already she is all about making something overwhelming into something manageable… we are on to a good start.

If you have seen Sheryl's name somewhere before, it might be because she has already been mentioned in this book – she backed our Crowdfunder campaign to get this book published. She's also what I lovingly call a "Good Egg". She's one of those lovely people who will try to help anyone. If you need help managing your critic, read the book and then ask her for help if you need it!

Despite being lovely, she is someone who's backside I kicked a little while ago. Seriously if I think you could easily get hacked – I'll tell you! And I'll annoy you as much as you will let me.

And hopefully you will do something about it…

The following is what Sheryl wanted to say.

Why don't I change even when I know better?

I had known Paul for a number of years, and he came across as a sincere and funny guy, so I naturally liked listening to him. It was only when I heard his 20-minute talk called MentalTheft, that I realised he was so much more than just a magician. Despite being inspired and impressed in equal measure I observed myself taking no action.

Being that my thing is making sense of why we say one thing and do another, I started to get curious about what was happening and why wasn't I motivated to act on his advice. This is a synopsis what happened in between thoughts and action. I hope by sharing it, you might be curious about what is happening for you and in doing so you will find your own way to make the changes needed to stay safe.

One of the many things I knew I needed to change was the way I was managing and creating my passwords. I had known long before listening to Paul that it was not a good thing to be using the same password in too many places. Especially if the password chosen was not particularly 'strong' in the first place. What became obvious almost instantly was a feeling of overwhelm. The change felt too big and there were too many variables and things that could go wrong. As I listened to my thoughts and feelings, I heard myself thinking that it was like a massive brick wall. As I explored what kind of brick wall, there were in fact three things blocking my thinking:

Safety, Confidence, Trust.

SAFETY

By admitting that Paul was right, that meant I had to admit that the ideal world I wanted to live in doesn't exist. I had to step out of my imaginary world that is full of love, kindness and trust and step into 'that' world. That instantly made me feel sad, unsafe and reticent to move. I didn't want Paul's reality to become my reality.

One thing that really helped is talking to Paul again. He is a genuinely lovely guy who cares passionately about others and lives a humble life himself. It was when I focused on his moral compass, I realised that he lived in 'that' world with those not so nice people and was still happy. That gave me hope and courage that I could protect myself and those that matter to me and still be open, loving and caring.

When I started to think about the people that really mattered to me and what would happen if they were wronged or hurt by one of the scams, I discovered a drive deep inside to make it happen. It fuelled the motivation to get out of my own way and make this change happen.

But I still got stuck. Despite being a highly motivated and organised person, I found myself camouflaging my inactivity with stories of priorities and business but that was just the story I told myself to justify my behaviour.

I am not proud to say that I had had the same four passwords used in various formats across all my technology. Alright, I changed the odd letter to a capital or number and added an exclamation mark here and there, but in essence if you had one of my passwords you could probably work out any of the others. I knew none of the passwords were particularly strong because nearly every system told me so.

The work involved to change felt harder and scarier and was imminent whereas the possibility that I could, maybe, one day get scammed seemed far away and not likely.

Not changing meant I didn't need to do anything. I didn't need to invest time creating and then remembering the new passwords. I didn't have to deal with the time and energy required to notify my team and my husband who also needed to access some of the same software associated with those passwords.

CONFIDENCE

Paul said you 'just' had to use software to securely store your passwords and it would even generate them for you.

When someone says 'just' and I already know I don't find it easy I can sometimes fall in the trap of putting myself down and saying things like "everyone else finds this kind of thing easy but I can't."

Once I recognised this was about my confidence to learn something new, I took a deep breath and decided to 'just' get started and have a go. I wish I could report to you that it was as easy and as smooth as Paul had suggested but it was not.

TRUST

I liked the idea of having really secure passwords and it scared me a little that a computer would generate them not me. I remember feeling weird that the password was not something that I associated with and instead was a random sequence of letters, numbers and symbols. I did not like the idea that I did not actually know my own passwords which would mean I would not be able to recall them or share them without looking them up.

As I explored that feeling it was about trust. It left me feeling out of control and like someone else had access to all my stuff, but I didn't. Once I got my head around the idea that the passwords were not 'my' passwords and that meant that they were super safe, I was able to move on to the next thought.

What is scary to admit is at the time of writing this, my web designer had my password for the website, and it was the same as the one for the business bank account. It makes me cringe with shame as I say it out loud, but it was *the truth. So, on some level I trusted my team more than I trusted myself to generate, retain and be able to access the random passwords.*

I felt embarrassment and shame for how long I had been ignoring this problem and what worked for me was to accept that this was about to become a story I could laugh about. It was going to shift from what I am doing, to what I was doing. That felt good to know it was not going to be how I did things from now on. I knew once I had done the work I could look back and laugh at this moment and appreciate the lesson.

I hope that hearing my story makes you feel less alone and that you will also do a little soul searching and work out what needs to happen for you to make the change. It was about this time when I really owned the fact that this change was happening and this old way of doing things was going to be ditched that my brain had what I loving call a 'brain fart'.

How big was this problem?

How many passwords am I talking about?

Which are the most important if I cannot do them all today?

What will the impact be on the business as I am just about to go away on holiday for three weeks?

…Were just some of the questions I started to ask myself.

I was committed to the change now. It was going to happen and even though I was just about to go on holiday for three weeks I was still one hundred percent committed. I had my why. I was doing this for myself and my loved ones. I wanted to be a good role model to my children, and I wanted to be a good role model to my clients.

BUT WHERE TO START?

I knew I needed to have a clear step by step plan that I could pick up and put down in between other tasks and responsibilities. I usually work this out by thinking about what is the first thing that needs to happen? Then what happens? Then what happens? Once I know the series of actions that will get me from where I am now, to where I want to be, I can then plan time to take action.

Sometimes the first step is – find myself a good teacher or someone that can do it for me. But being passwords, this job had to be done by me.

This is the process that I mapped out:
1. *List all the software that I needed to change the password for.*
2. *Prioritise which were the most important to change before my holiday*
3. *Make sure I did not change anything my PA needed while I was away.*
4. *Learn how the app works on my laptop to generate passwords for me.*
5. *Find a secure way to share the new passwords with my team.*
6. *Let my husband know how to access it should anything happen to me.*

In a busy day it was easy to want to park it and forget it. It was easier to talk about it and even write this article about what I was thinking than actually doing the work. But the process mapped out gave me clarity and focus and so I took action. I listed my passwords. There were 14 that I was instantly aware of and suddenly it didn't seem like such a big job.

I would like to say that this meant I was highly motivated. But instead, I found myself distracting myself once again. That is when I pulled myself back to the process. What is the next thing that needs to happen? The next step was to prioritise. In my head I had already forgotten that and was busying my mind with learning how to use the new system. Once I caught that thought I brought myself back to the next step in the process and got on with prioritising.

The moment of truth came. Now I had to face my demons and learn how to use this new system. I signed up with Lastpass per Pauls recommendation and got started. Please don't roll your eyes but when asked for a password as my master password guess which password I wanted to use. Yep my default favourite. The one I remembered easily.

But of course, that was not going to work. That was the whole point of setting this system up. I am pleased to say that I created a new password and for a day or two I did have it written down by my side and I had to type it in several times to embed it. Yes, I did forget it. Yes, I did get in a panic but eventually I got the hang of the master password. That was not before I locked myself out of my bank account and my credit card and several other accounts.

Every time it happened, I found myself having to count to ten and remind myself that I have got this and despite the discomfort this was nothing compared to how bad it would be if I got hacked.

I should point out at this point that I have been hacked before so there is plenty of evidence that my systems were not secure enough. I have had someone buy a new watch using my bank details years ago, I have had my bank account emptied and someone decided to host porn on the home page of my website.

Due to the efficiency of my bank and my website hosting company none of them really caused me sufficient discomfort which was something I had to overcome as the discomfort of change was much more painful than my previous experience of being scammed.

Paul explained that banks are getting a little fed up with always being liable and that they are getting better at sharing the responsibility to verify. Therefore, it was more likely in the future I would be liable and I would not get my money back.

CONFIDENCE

Normally once I have committed to change, I take action. But sometimes when I am on the fence with a decision it can be just one person's comment or even lack of comment that can knock my confidence. Or it can be a few silly setbacks, like being locked out that can make me want to give up.

I remember talking to my husband briefly in between clients about the tool I was using and he instantly said, "it sounds suspicious if it is in the cloud and free". He inferred that he would not put his passwords in that system and the impact was that I started to doubt my decision.

I told my husband that I really trusted Paul and so he took a look into the company and eventually said he thought it was okay. Without this follow up conversation and my unshakable belief in Paul it is likely that I would have got stuck yet again.

So, I got on and created my master password and felt suitably pleased that I was making progress. I loved that the system gave me a great big green light which indicated that it was a strong password.

I mean really strong; it is right to the end of the bar. It could not be any better. Then I am asked to click 'Get' and a warning appears that says:

"This extension can:
*   - read and change all the data on the websites you visit*
*   - display notifications"*

At which point I feel physically sick and feel like the invisible risk that something might happen is much easier to deal with than clicking this button and being told it is my fault that I gave some company access to my computer. The only thing that is keeping me going is that I trust Paul. I like Paul. Then the worse thing of all happens. I remember that most con men from the movies are pretty charming and lovely. What if I am being scammed? A follow up conversation with my hubby who works in IT reassures me that this warning is normal and typical for this kind of product and so I press click and it is done.

Well almost, the warning message comes up and says it could not connect with my server and I need to try again. Only now I have a call with clients, and I have to park this for now. But I am committed that this job will be finished today. It felt quite stressful. It has not been easy and at this point it would be easy to think I have wasted most of the day.

Instead, I take a moment to acknowledge the progress made. I may not have the 'whole' system up and running yet, but I do know the accounts I want to add to it. I also know for a few dollars per month I can share the password with my team, and I can give emergency access to the account and I am committed to take action until the change has happened. That is a massive shift from pretending I don't have to change.

I have a couple more hiccups which include not being able to find the login page, adding the wrong passwords and eventually locking myself out of my bank account and credit card just as the payments are due.

But eventually I get in.

Eventually after a few deep breaths and a little more patience I start to make sense of how the system works and eventually I am creating random passwords with confidence and before long I discover that I have over 50 passwords to be stored.

It feels great to finally have my affairs in order and a space to store everything for my loved ones should anything happen to me.

All in all, it took me several hours over several weeks, but I can honestly say that the system is actually saving me time now. I can't thank Paul enough for stepping up and sharing his wisdom.

If you are stuck and you are not sure why you don't change even if you know better, take a moment to really listen to your thoughts. Listen to what you say out loud and what you mutter under your breath. The clues are there when you really listen. Once you know why you are not taking action you are one step closer to finding a way that works for you.

Paul's reaction to Sheryl's story

I read this piece and it amazed me. It amazed me because I know Sheryl as a person who always seems confident in what she does and is an absolute master in doing it. She has everything nailed and has a lovely way of putting people at ease to make difficult tasks seem really easy to work through. For her to put together this piece which shows a level of worry that I never thought she would have was just amazing! It has also made me question a few things about my delivery of projects and my lack of worry ability.

I've always known that myself and my family have a weird reaction to stressful situations, we tend to breeze through them, not showing any worry, fear or doubt and then after a scary situation has passed, we would look at each other and say things like "well that was close" or "that was a bit of a situation" and my dad would just "deal with something" and move on. He never (from what I remember) shows any fear and that really has carried over to myself and my brother.

I honestly think that is a massive part of why I can steal someone's wallet from them without batting an eyelid. (PS – if you want lessons on how to do that I know just the man!)

So here is an apology from me.

If I make something look too easy, please understand that it may take a bit more time, effort and planning than I am 100% showing you. But I promise you this. It will be worth it.

Sheryl has taken a massive step toward making herself and her family more protected from scammers, which will make her feel more confident about her situation AND make her finances more stable.

Because here's the bit I can never quantify – the horrible feeling of knowing you can't pay your bills, can't pay for petrol or travel to your next job, can't even buy the food you need at the supermarket. Because some scammer has either taken all of your cash, or stolen your credit cards so they had to be cancelled. It's a horrendous feeling that I've watched too many friends go through.

Password managers

I was a bit worried about how to address password protection tools. I talked about PINs and biometrics, Jesse also started talking about biometrics, and I knew that if I jumped into online tools you were going to stop reading! But, thanks to Sheryl covering most of the points, I hope you can see that it something you should be looking at.

The reality is that in the modern world, the more different and complex passwords you have for your different accounts, the safer you are. I see news stories almost every day about one company or other who has had a data breach. Well if your smart watch account is hacked, and the password and email address is the same as your bank and email and website, etc, you are going to be in trouble!

It is not as difficult as you would think to test thousands of account details to see if their details log you into other accounts. I asked Jesse for one of his explanations here and he babbled on about scripts, SQL, bots and algorithms (I might be making some of those words up?), but all I know is he started it with "oh yeah, it would be really easy to…". Yeah, I am not letting him have a bubble here, but let's just say you don't want to risk it. So, what is the advice?

The advice is to use a Password Manager, such as LastPass, Dashlane or RoboForm (others probably exist, but these are ones that I am aware of). The idea is that you give these tools access to log onto your account – that is to say you give it your email address and password. It then does a number of things:

- Changes your password to something very secure
- Typically, it schedules changing that password regularly to make sure it stays secure

You heard the fear from Sheryl's story – and that is largely over the next bit – you never know what that password is. How it works is, you have access to the password manager – when you want to log into something, you use verification with your ONE SECURE PASSWORD to the verification manager, and it sorts out the rest. OK, I will let Jesse have a bubble to put your minds at rest…

Jesse's thoughts on password managers

I have talked to friends about password managers, and I understand that the basic concept does not seem that safe – so why do people like Paul, and indeed cyber security experts swear by them? Firstly, with your existing password, it is stored by the people you are signing into. You hear of pretty much every big online company having data breaches, making your email and password at risk – your password is stored everywhere online already, and it's getting stolen.

Secondly, you think you know what your password is, because that's what you type onto the screen. The reality is that it is converted and encrypted and changed from all recognition before it flies around the internet. You have no idea what any of that is, or what it means or how it happens. Not knowing the bit on the screen is only one less bit you don't know!

Password Manager companies are doing one job, and that is keeping things safe. They employ top technology, and by its very nature, is changing your passwords when things get hacked. Even if their data was stolen, the worst thing you would have to do is change your one high quality password.

And if you are still not sure, I say to you this. If you're not sure and don't understand, ask more experts. They will either agree with us – in which case that's probably a good way to go, or they will disagree and you will have to research and make your own mind up! Seriously, ask around.

Phishing emails

Phishing emails is a fancy term for scam emails that get sent to a lot of people. Imagine going fishing, taking your rod and casting into a lake hoping to catch a fish. The scammers send emails out to thousands of people to try and trick any percentage of them. There is one famous one, which is a version of the Spanish Prisoner, so let's start here.

The Spanish Prisoner

This scam sounds so fanciful, it's crazy that anyone ever falls for it, but they do. The Spanish Prisoner con is one of the oldest tricks in the book, originating around the 16th century. The scammer claims to be an aristocrat who is being held in a faraway land under a false name. They need bail money and can't reveal their true identity. If you help, you'll be rewarded with riches and diplomatic favours. Complications soon arise, and the poor soul needs more money. Victims hand over cash until they get suspicious or run out of money.

This scam is more popularly known today as the Nigerian Prince, due to the subject of phishing emails. In this version, a person posing as a relative of an African royal or diplomat pretends to need money for an expensive item being kept in a warehouse. The item will be extremely valuable and worth more than the fee to recover it. The scammer promises to reward your generosity by depositing a significant amount of money into your account. Before that happens, you have to pay fees so that they can pay bribes or ransom to officials. They may claim that the officials want US or UK money because it's worth more. Ignore these stories — just leave those rich prisoners in Spain.

Getting clever

The Nigerian Prince email is our starting point because it is so famous now that it just seems absurd. However, the scammers are getting more and more sophisticated. Almost every day I receive an email that looks like it is from a bank, or from an online shopping site such as Amazon or EBAY. They typically try to incite varying levels of fear, to get you to click on a link. Often, they will take you to a spoof website where they will try to get you to insert details that will be used to scam you. Alternatively, those links will download malware (bad software) or viruses that will do anything from breaking your computer to reading what you are typing so they can see your passwords when you log in to different websites.

The key is to be wary of these emails – it is always better to be safe and delete them than click on them "just in case". If you are not sure, call the company – they will very often be glad that you have reported the scam email to them. If you are not expecting to hear from whoever it is, then you probably aren't hearing from them.

Ghost insurance

I'm currently doing a fair bit of work with insurance companies. The thought behind this is the more that we can teach the brokers and their clients, then the less fraud will be committed and therefore the less insurance companies will have to pay out. This will also lead to premiums getting cheaper and better value, so I'm more than happy to assist in this way of thinking.

This scam was pointed out to me by one of those brokers. He is someone who actually cares that his clients are well looked after, which means that I was immediately interested in what he had to say.

What is Ghost insurance? You go to search for a new insurance policy online and you find a company that is offering a massive 30% off for new customers and it's promotional offer looks like it could save you a massive amount from your last policy.

You shop around a bit but no one else is even coming close AND they are even adding in some extras like "Solicitor fees covered for any claim" or "No claims bonus stays intact even if you make 2 claims in that year!" If you go ahead, and your policy is received really quickly. All looks great and you feel happy with what you've got. But here's the problem.

They didn't insure YOU. They got a real policy, BUT instead of insuring you at your address with your details they've insured some little old lady at an address that is so remote that no one would ever visit the let alone burgle them. They then doctored the policy so it all looks great and has all of your details. This can be done thousands of times just by using the lure of an internet cheap price. And unless you make a claim, you'll never know.

Something else to think about is this – to get that policy you just told a scammer ALL of your personal details. Real personal data fetches a decent price on the black market, and the more that people sell good data, the more they can charge for it – it's like getting an EBAY seller rating!

Not only are you at risk because you have paid money, but are not actually insured (which has many implications, such as voiding other contracts or breaking laws), but you are now at risk because it is really easy to steal your identity and hack your accounts. Here you can see the three forms of Mental Theft coming together:

- Belief – you believed they were a real credit broker
- The Steal – they took your money
- Placement – With your personal details they have access to everything

This last one might not be that clear yet, because you are clever and used a different password – they don't know the password to your bank account, for example. But you paid the scammer money, so they know where you bank. It doesn't take long to go through a bank helpline to get someone to help you with an issue using their service. If you have a maiden name, a phone number, a date of birth, an address – which you gave willingly to the Ghost Insurance company – you will likely have gotten through the door.

"Oh, btw friendly bank person, can I change my email address? And my mobile number has changed. And my contact address – a lot has changed; I have just moved to a new house!"

Oops.

The best advice I can give here is to use known and trusted sites if doing comparisons. Better still to use a broker that you know personally! It may cost you a bit more but let's be honest. If you need to make a claim, you want it to pay out don't you?

Microsoft call

This one is getting to the point of being farcical – it's happening so often that people are talking about it in the pub or in the restaurants when they meet up with friends. Your phone rings at home and you answer it.

"Hello madam, this is Dave from Microsoft, we are calling to let you know that there seems to be a problem with your computer and we need to fix it as soon as possible!" You probably know someone who has had this call? Or you've similar yourself? What they want you to do is turn on your computer and download a specific program, or go to a specific website.

Once you are on this program or website, they will helpfully get you to give them control of your machine. They can then do various things with it. They can find any banking information you've left on there. They will definitely search your machine for the word "password". They may put a trojan horse onto your computer which will constantly update them with everything your computer is doing. At the very least they will restrict access to your machine and charge you a fee to regain access.

The way to beat this one is simple – Don't believe them!

Why would Microsoft or your internet provider be calling you in the first place? If there's a problem with your computer you need to go to a trusted person to get it fixed NOT to some random person who called your home phone!

My dad is amazing at dealing with these people, he truly dislikes computers and whenever he gets these phones call, he purposely winds them up for as long as possible! Well done dad, because while you're annoying these scammers, they can't be scamming someone else.

Gone fishing! Catfishing to be exact...

Catfishing is when someone sets up a fake profile online to start a relationship with someone, with the aim to scam money or personal information out of them. There are a lot of these profiles within online dating BUT you can even find them in places like LinkedIn!

We recently did an interview with Erica Mackay on our podcast show, Newton's Nuggets. In her business, The Marketing Detective Agency, she works on understanding human nature and using it to help businesses to build a robust marketing strategy. Jesse and Erica could probably talk marketing all day, but that's not why she was talking to MentalTheft. As well as her business, Erica immerses herself in social media, where she finds catfishes and plays with them online!

She puts out personas where she gets targeted by catfishes, and runs through the process, not just to target them, but to understand how they work and what it is that they try to achieve.

The reality is that they prey on specific people – and they work in volume. If they can target 1000 people and a handful respond, they have done well. They try to build a romance, so that you fall hopelessly in love with them. For some, this far-away kind of love seems weird and not believable. But, if you are lonely and single, a catfish is probably providing a lot of positive emotions, which is what draws you in. And even if they don't ask for money, we tell our partners everything, and once you have it is easy to scam you.

But meeting people online is a normal part of life these days, so how do you make sure you swipe left on a catfish?

Erica has told us some signs that someone might be a catfish, because to those who have been drawn in, it is not always obvious to look for the bad points. The first thing anyone should do when starting a relationship someone is to look them up online. It always used to be called cyber stalking, but we have so much stuff online nowadays, looking people up is a way of life.

Do a search of their name on the internet and across social media. Do they exist? Do their photos match across their profiles.

A key sign of a catfish is the thing that draws a lot of people in – too much affection too soon. If they start telling you they love you really quickly, that often draws people in, but that is a good sign to start being wary.

Very often, a catfish will avoid face-to-face chats such as video calls and certainly won't meet in person. In this modern world where we are all used to video calling, if they are saying no, be very careful.

Jesse's trick with image search

A tool a lot of people don't know about is Google's search by image function. Go to the home screen of google, and in the top right, next to your profile button and the Gmail button is an Images link.

From here you can do two searches. The first – search for the person's name… The reality is, it is hit and miss on here whether you get any search results doing this – normally there are thousands of people with the same name. However, if you have a picture of someone, save it, and click the camera icon to search by image.

From here you can upload the image and see where it appears on the internet. If google finds the same image against other people, you have a high chance that this is a scammer.

One thing that Erica said that I thought is really interesting is the fact that there are always excuses for things like not meeting up, not being able to answer etc. They are often elaborate stories, things like "I am in the military and I am deployed on a mission". But after a while, the stories can conflict with each other, because at the end of the day, a catfish is trying to do this with a lot of people, and so are trying to remember where they are in different relationships.

Which brings us on to the next interesting fact. This isn't a case of day 1 contact, day 3 I love you, day 7 can I have some money. Catfish will often work for months on a relationship, which is why they have an excuse for not being there for months – it adds longevity to the relationship without them having to make up more lies.

Catfishing can really tear people apart. It's a horrible scam that preys on people's wants and need to be loved. Stay wary, and if you get any signs that don't seem right, check them out. There is a checklist for catfish in the checklist section.

You know, but does your family know?

I started writing this book by telling you why – because not everyone will see my show and I need to get the information out there. I am passing the baton on to you – with great knowledge comes great responsibility. Start at home – make sure you are keeping an eye on your children, educating them in how to be careful. Don't assume because someone is smart that they know and understand the risks – many very clever business leaders find their businesses hacked!

My number one aim is to keep as many people as safe as possible. So please protect your family. Keep them informed, and if necessary, put in place safeguards.

Chapter 4
In Your Home

Technology is not the only way that scammers can reach you in your own home. People are so worried about things such as internet security that we must not forget that there are other parts of our lives that are at risk from fraudsters and scammers. The homes we live in are often forgotten about, and with increasing reports of crime such as burglary, we need to think about security.

Most home security issues can be improved quickly and cheaply, and will put your mind at rest. I put together a checklist, but Jesse said it was too boring to read, so we have put the checklist in the checklist chapter! To talk about home security, I went to a friend in the sector, Diane Ivory. These days, Diane is often found doing talks, and setting up CSI events for business teamworking or as fun hen parties! But she a former Scotland Yard and Metropolitan Police fingerprint expert and crime scene examiner.

In fact, Diane is the real world CSI, with over 29 years' experience crime solving across London, Norfolk and Suffolk. She has some incredible stories, from the very interesting to the very bizarre to the downright scary! I asked her about security, and she said, there is no such thing as 100% secure, you can just make your home more difficult than other people's. Sounds familiar, that's what we have been saying about cyber security as well…

So we asked her how we do that, and we think her title was rather apt!

How to make a burglar visit your neighbour instead of you!

Burglary: The "Illegal entry of a building with intent to commit a crime, especially theft".

I am a former Scotland Yard Fingerprint Expert and CSI and spent nearly 30 years examining all types of crime scenes for fingerprints and other physical trace evidence. I compared finger marks recovered to identify those who had left their fingerprints behind.

I have been to thousands of burglaries so have learnt a thing or 2 about the way burglars work and how to avoid them paying you a visit.

I have also met thousands of people who have been burgled and witnessed their reactions to it.

I have lost count of the number of times I was asked "why me?" My first thoughts were usually "do you really want to me to tell you?"

I could swerve answering as I had the more gentle cop out of suggesting they get in touch with the Crime Prevention Officer and ask them to visit to suggest ways to make their homes more secure to avoid being burgled again. Today you might have a visit from someone working with the Safer Neighbourhood Team who could give you some advice. Worth a chat for sure.

I totally understand the feelings victims of burglary experience as I have been burgled myself. It may seem odd, but whilst terrible at the time, there was a great benefit to me having been burgled. It meant I could genuinely empathise with the people I was there to help. I don't think you can really understand the full impact of a burglary unless you've experienced it yourself.

It is a horrible experience.

I hated the fact that someone I didn't know had walked around my house unseen and uninvited.

I hated that they had opened drawers and cupboards and taken some of my most treasured possessions.

I hated the mess they had left in their wake and that it was me who had to clear it up.

I hated that they knew what I had and the uncertainty of if they would return to take it?

Ultimately, I hated that they got away with it and were likely to go on to burgle many more homes. Sadly, there will always be people who will steal from others.

I am going to help you with some top tips so that you can make your neighbour's house, or if not your direct neighbour, another nearby property, be a far more appealing proposition to break into than you and in so doing, avoid being a victim of burglary yourself.

You need to ensure that you are not an easy nor obvious target for burglary. Take a good look at your property and make the changes that are needed to make a burglar go elsewhere.

Outside Appearance

Let's start with the perimeter.

You may have acres of land, a small yard or something in between. Either way, there will be a boundary to your property. Most properties have some sort of barrier marking these boundary lines which run at the front, side and rear of your property.

Most often the boundary will be marked by a fence, wall or hedge/plants. It might be even be a stream. Whatever it is, you need to make it difficult to get through.

Spend a bit of time looking at your perimeter with the eyes of a potential intruder and fix anything that you feel makes you vulnerable.

Fences - Keep them in good repair. If they are collapsing or have missing panels, they will make you an easy target.

I am often asked if it is legal to fix carpet gripper rods to the top of fences. Whilst it is not illegal to do so, someone may have a claim against you if they injure themselves on them whilst climbing over. Most burglars are wise to this practise anyway and would most likely put a jumper or bag on the spikes so they could scale it unharmed.

Hedging and plants – It is less easy to climb over a hedge than a fence as it is not so stable. The higher the hedge, the harder it is, but please consider that you want to keep this hedge looking tidy which will involve more work than a fence or wall.

Planting a prickly hedge isn't a bad idea. Kind of nature's equivalent to fixing carpet gripper rod to the top of a fence. You'd certainly know about it if you landed in a holly bush!

Walls – a good solid wall can act as a fantastic obstacle. It can't be peered through in the way fencing or plants might be, and if tall enough, can't easily be seen over. Any potential intruder would be taking a big risk of being seen as soon as they scaled it and dropped into the garden beyond. Who knows, you could have the local SNT officer in your garden giving you some advice on security when a would be burglar drops in on you!

Nothing – I know of many properties that don't have any type of physical boundary. These are mostly in the country where the neighbouring property is a field and the homeowner wants an uninterrupted view of the countryside surrounding them. In these cases it will be easy to gain access to the land your property stands in, so it's advisable to really concentrate on getting the best security you can to stop anyone gaining access to the property itself. Many countryside properties have quite extensive land with no close neighbours, so there will be less likelihood of anyone seeing and reporting an intruder than in say, a terraced property in the city.

Do not ignore the front of your house. This often gives a good picture of the occupant.

For example, an overgrown and messy garden with faded curtains at the window might suggest that an elderly person is living there.

Sadly, there are some burglars who prey on older people and trick their way into houses with the intention to steal. If you have elderly friends or relatives who are unable to tend to their garden offer to help them out with a spot of gardening and warn them of the dangers of allowing strangers into their home.

It is not unusual for people to claim to need to enter a premises because there is a problem with the water/gas/electricity etc. It's not just the elderly who are taken in by these people, so please, everyone be alert and if in any doubt, don't let anyone in unless you are confident they are who they say they are and have a legitimate reason to be there.

Anyone who is genuine will understand if you want to shut the door on them while you call the company they claim to be from to check they are there for the reasons they say they are.

You may have heard about, or seen for yourself, chalk marks drawn on the pavement outside some houses. Gangs often work together, with some members going out to scope an area, and leave written "codes" in chalk on the pavement for others in the gang to follow.

Amongst other things, the chalk marks might indicate that there is a dog in the house, that the house is unoccupied or that the householder is elderly. If you see these marks and are concerned, take photographs, alert the police, and wash the chalk away.

Window Shopping

Another thing to consider is what you are advertising through your windows. Can someone passing by look in the window and see what you have that they might like to have themselves?

There have been many times when I have examined the outside surfaces of windows and found finger marks, lip marks, nose marks and even ear marks. These have been left behind by people who have been up close and looking in and listening at the windows. They are looking to see if anyone is in and to see what they can aim to grab once they are inside.

Do not leave valuable items on display. Your windows should not provide a window-shopping opportunity for potential burglars. Laptops, phones, cameras, gaming consoles etc. are all items that may easily be seen through a window. Make them less visible and get in the habit of hiding them if you can *when the house is unoccupied.*

Here's something many of us, including me, are guilty of...

Think about when you return home after a day out. What do you do with your bags? Your wallet? Your keys?

Many of us just dump them where they land. On the floor in the hall. On the table. On the stairs.

IF you don't move these later and they are visible through windows, or even glass panels in your front door if you have them, they will be easy targets to take.

I have examined many residential burglaries where a car has also been stolen. Make it difficult for this to happen to you. Do not leave the car keys where they can be found. Simple!

From today onwards, think about where what you take back into the house with you when you return home lands. Is there a better place to leave it? Somewhere where it can't be seen so easily? Somewhere where it can't be grabbed so easily?

Security
We have taken care of the appearance of the outside of your property and what is inside being visible from the outside, now we need to look at your security.

In simple terms you need to make it as difficult as possible to gain access, and as I said before, to make it look like it's going to be much easier to burgle your neighbour.

Cameras and Alarms

If there is a chance that someone is going to be filmed whilst on your property it might make them reluctant to even attempt to gain access.

Sometimes just a sign to alert people to the fact that they are being filmed could be all the deterrent that is needed. You may not even need a camera. You could install a convincing dummy camera to act as a deterrent.

Obviously, if this doesn't act as a deterrent and someone really does attempt to gain entry you might kick yourself for not installing a real camera that could have filmed them in the act. This provides excellent evidence when trying to identify the intruder which in turn, gives you a better chance of recovering any property that has been stolen.

Alarms can be a great deterrent too. Whilst they may not stop people entering, if an alarm goes off whilst someone is on site, they are likely to leave pretty quickly, taking less with them than they would if they had more time.

This is great example of why you should leave as little as possible in site and easily accessible. There are many homes that are burgled and "only" a handbag is taken. That is because the bag was dumped in the hall/on the table/on the stairs and was grabbed just as the alarm activated and before the intruder had time to search elsewhere.

Losing a handbag is a nightmare. It's not just having to replace anything valuable that was in it, but it's also having to cancel cards that were in the purse. Replace the makeup in the makeup bag. Figure out what your plans for the next who knows how long are, because your diary/notebook/tablet etc were also in there. Not to mention that dear little key ring that your kids made you when they were in kindergarten 10 years ago. You see where I'm going with this.

Lights

It could be argued that lights serve to help a potential intruder see what they are doing as they attempt to gain entry. However, if someone triggers a light sensor while you are inside and your garden becomes lit up like the Blackpool Illuminations, you may well see from inside that the lights have gone on and you can go and investigate.

Where you can, set the sensor so that pets and wildlife are unlikely to trigger them or you'll be up and down all night looking at our furry friends and may get to the stage where every time you look it's an animal, so the one time it's a real intruder you don't bother getting up to look.

Of course, if you have CCTV cameras installed, the lights will alert you to look at your monitor and will enable a much clearer picture of the intruder.

This is important and worthy of capitals - IF YOU HAVE AN ALARM, CCTV OR LIGHTS, THEY ARE USELESS UNLESS YOU TURN THEM ON!

I lost count of the number of householders who had been burgled and told me they hadn't turned the alarm on because they "weren't going to be out for long" or that they'd "only nipped to the shops".

I know that not everyone has contents insurance for their home, but if you do, it is worth checking the terms of your policy. If you have told the insurance company that you have an alarm and then don't activate it you may not be covered for any losses incurred.

I have a friend who fell foul to this clause when she had left the house to work in her garden. She had locked the doors but had not set the alarm. When someone broke in while she was in the garden the insurance company refused to pay up.

Locks

Like alarms, lights and CCTV, locks are only worthwhile if YOU TURN THE KEY.

Again, check your insurance policy. It may stipulate that locks need to be of a certain type and the window or door that they secure is locked for you to be able to make a claim for any losses.

Many modern doors and windows come with integral locks fitted. You just need to turn the key and many bolts slide into place at various intervals around the closing.

Older style doors and windows will require locks to be fitted to them and it is worth seeking professional help to determine which would be the best lock for your situation.

Things to consider:

• The positioning of locks and having more than one lock on a door.
• Do not leave keys in the lock. It is not unheard of for burglars to insert something from the outside that will turn the key on the inside.
• Do not leave keys visible from the outside. Burglars are not stupid. They can be very clever and have been known to use something to reach through the letterbox to hook the keys they can see, pull them back through the letter box then use them to undo the lock.
• Be mindful of who you give your keys to.
• MAKE SURE YOU CAN GET OUT IF THERE IS A FIRE – Keep your property safe from intruders, but please ensure that keys are easily accessible to you when you are in your home. IF there is a fire and you need to escape you don't want to be stopped by a locked door or window.

This is important and worthy of repetition and capitals – YOUR LOCKS ARE USELESS UNLESS YOU HAVE TURNED THE KEY TO LOCK THEM.

Common Sense

Here's a few little extras that are really just common sense, but sometimes we get caught up with "stuff" and our common sense falls by the wayside for a while. I'll list a few things to think about.

I hope that none of them will be a surprise and that you'll be shouting at me for telling you something that's obvious and you would already consider:

- *If you're going to be away from home for holiday/work/hospital stays etc. don't advertise that you're away on social media.*
- *Don't let anyone overhear you telling your friends in the street or down the pub that you're going to be away and that the house will be empty.*
- *Cancel any regular deliveries you have before you go away.*
- *If you are going away and your usually full driveway is going to be empty, ask your neighbours if they could park on it for you till you get back.*
- *Use time switches for lights/curtains – if you can, make it look as though you are at home even when you are not by having the lights come on and windows covered. If you don't have the means to do it automatically, ask a friend or neighbour to do it for you.*

Best of all, if you are going to be away for a while, consider asking someone to house sit for you.

You've just bought yourself a brand-new Rolex/high spec phone/swanky set of golf clubs. Lovely. Make sure you enjoy them for longer by not shouting about it and posting pictures all over social media.

Keep your bank cards safe. If you mislay any you can usually use your banking app to put a stop on them till you find them. If you don't find them you need to cancel them as soon as possible.

Burn, or use a shredder to destroy confidential personal information rather than putting it in the recycling bin.

If you hide things of value in your house (many people do) make sure that someone you trust knows where your hiding places are. It's no good thinking you're smart hiding the family jewels in a block of ice in the freezer if no one knows you've done it. If something happens to you and you've not told a trusted family member where to find them there's a good chance they'll never be found when your house is being cleared.

LOCK YOUR DOORS
TURN ON YOUR ALARM
SET THE CCTV TO RECORD

This is just a snippet of things to think about and I really hope it has got you thinking. I am sure you will come up with loads of things I've missed.

I have concentrated on residential burglaries only, but the same considerations should be given to business and commercial premises, outbuildings and vehicles.

The title to this chapter suggests that you should make your home a less attractive proposition to burgle than your neighbours.

In the spirit of kindness I'd love it if having made your home one that burglars would avoid that you help your neighbours to do the same with theirs. Wouldn't it be great to live in a street where burglars don't bother visiting as it's not worth their while.

If you see something suspicious, report it. Police would far rather be called out to a genuine false alarm than deal with the aftermath of a crime. If you return home or wake in the night and suspect that someone is in your house, dial 999 and tell the Police that you think there is an intruder on site. Don't be big and brave and go looking for them yourself. This is how a "burglary" can become an "aggravated burglary".

I'll leave you with the words of the late Shaw Taylor who used to host the TV crime show Police 5 - Keep 'em peeled.

Make your own property safe and be vigilant.

Paul's Thoughts on Home Security

Many thanks to Diane, what an in-depth look into home security. If, like me you found that extremely interesting, but have no idea where to start, don't worry, the checklists come later, and they will really help.

But burglars are not the only risk in your home. As well as cybersecurity, where can the scam be coming from?

Your Doorstep

A doorstep scam is where a person knocks on your door and tries to either scam you out of money OR tries to gain access to your home.

We sometimes come up with the idea of a pushy or stereotypical nasty type of person at our door, but they can often be very nice, polite and friendly. The first lesson is that if you're not expecting someone at your door then it's worth being wary, especially if you're on your own!

Please don't think that only stupid people can fall for doorstep scams, I know some very intelligent people who have fallen for some of these scams. But what does a doorstep scam look like – how do we spot it?

What are some common types of doorstep scams?

There are many different types of doorstep scams, some of the most common ones include:

Rogue traders

A cold caller offering you a service or trade that you don't actually need. In essence, it's hard to see this as a scam, as you are essentially paying for work; they will offer to fix a hazardous issue in your garden or even on your roof. This is usually done by using fear, getting sued by people getting hurt, or getting fined for meeting regulations. This is normally done in such a way to try and make you make a quick decision.

Fake visitors

Claiming to be from a utility company can be a great way to gain access to your home. In the workmen scam, con artists posing as gas, water, or electric company employees come to your house to check on a suspected leak or shortage. They instruct you to turn on some control panel in the basement or go outside and tell them when something changes, but this is simply a distraction, allowing them to loot your house.

This scam is easy to pull off for a bold scammer, but it's even easier to avoid by always checking the credentials of any purported utility company employees. ALWAYS ask for ID, if they are real, they will have no problem with you verifying their information – find a number online (not a number they give you) to phone and verify if you are not sure. If they're a scammer they will hate this! Real employees have identification, drive marked vehicles, and won't mind you calling to verify their claims. If they complain or insist on entering, lock your door and alert the police.

Fake charity

Someone may pretend to be from a charity to ask for money, clothes or items as a donation! This one can be a knock on the door or even an envelope through your letter box, asking you to leave the items outside. Why waste a good scammers time talking to someone when a little flyer and a free bag can do all the work for them?! Legitimate charities have a charity number that can be verified, so make sure you investigate who you are giving things to.

Consumer surveys

Fancy completing a survey for this nice person? Why not, its just a bit of your time? Whilst you are answering the questions, you are at the same time potentially giving them lots of your personal information that they can use elsewhere. I know of one scammer who was pretending to do a survey but at the end he was asking people to sign a document to prove he had been there – the document was actually a contract for services that the homeowner knew nothing about! Be careful of giving personal details to strangers, and be VERY wary about signing anything.

Tough luck story

Someone may come to your door and ask you to help them out. They may ask for cash, or they may ask to use your telephone or claim they're feeling unwell. The truth is they're probably just trying to find out information or gain access to your house. Be very careful, especially if you are on your own. If they need to call someone, take the details, lock the door and call for them.

How do I stop these scams??

There are loads of things you can do – and this is in no way all of them!

Sod off sign

You know the ones – it says something like "We don't want any cold callers or any salespeople to knock on the door." These are particularly effective if you say that you are an NHS worker working shifts – people are often more reluctant to annoy NHS workers, and the irregular working hours can put people off because they don't know whether you are there or not. Cheeky plug time – we sell some of these on our shop, head over to www.mentaltheft.co.uk/shop.

Supplier passwords

You can quite easily request that any of your suppliers (Electric, gas, phone, water etc) have to use a password when visiting your property. This is something I would really like to see become normal as soon as possible. Call your suppliers to set it up!

Befriend a neighbour

I know this sounds silly, but every neighbourhood would be so much better if we all looked out for each other. If you are going to answer the door to someone, could you call a neighbour to stay on the phone with you while you see who it is?

Panic Alarms

I don't really like panic alarms, but they serve a purpose! If you or someone you know, is in any way vulnerable, then a panic alarm hanging on a necklace or even hung next to the front door would scare most would be scammers away.

- If someone knocks on your door – REMEMBER:
- Only let someone in if you're expecting them! Or they're someone you know and trust
- Never be afraid to send someone away
- Don't feel pressured. Scammers love to use fear and pressure to force you into making a quick decision in their favour
- Check their ID. Ask for their ID, check it with the correct phone number (not necessarily the one they have given you! I know I've said it elsewhere but please – TRUST BUT VERIFY!
- Keep your PIN secret. No one else ever needs to know your PIN details. No one! EVER!
- Call the police. In the UK the police have a non-emergency number (101), if you're not happy with someone on, in or near your property please call them. If someone is causing you to feel fear, distress or danger in any way then please call the emergency number (in the UK it's 999!)

Scams through your letterbox!

Postal scams are getting better and better, and it can be tough to spot the difference between junk mail, scam mail and honest offers from your home service providers!

What are post scams?

Post scams come in many different forms and it's often hard to tell what is what. We're going to list some of them in the hope that it will help you spot them in the future!

Lotteries/prize draws

YOU'VE WON A PRIZE!!!! But hold on, you didn't enter a competition did you? Most of the time they'll ask you to call a premium rate phone line to collect your prize (at £something ridiculous per hour) or they will ask you to send the admin fee to them before you can receive your winnings of millions! Please don't respond to them – real lotteries will send you the prize without asking for anything from you in advance.

Psychics and clairvoyants

The psychic can see something coming in your future, but they need their fee before they will give you all of the amazing details! They sometimes work with the lottery scams to make it look like they knew about your upcoming good fortune!

AGAIN – Please don't respond! It may look like a very personal letter, but these are sent out to thousands of people every day.

Pyramid schemes

Pyramid schemes/Chain letters/Investment schemes that offer profits for little or no risk. They might want you to get others involved. Or, they'll tell you to send money to the person that told you about this?

Don't join! – if it seems too good to be true, it probably is. Pyramid schemes often involve overpriced products of no real value.

You may even receive a threat within the letter (could be along the lines of if you don't do this then there will be a hex on your family……) it's there to scare you into responding. Ignore it.

It is important at this point to note that there is a difference between a pyramid scheme and a Multi-Level Marketing (MLM) or direct marketing. There has been a massive surge in people getting involved with MLM companies and it is important to know the difference. An MLM is a way for companies to build up a network of representatives that sell their products for them.

There are many great ones of these (I used to do it!), we even interviewed Amy on our Newton's Nuggets podcast, who has been very successful through "Body Shop at Home". The key thing is that they are selling products. Pyramid schemes are based on investing money into the scheme and you can only make any money back by recruiting more people. Consider getting involved with anything like this like as if it were a proper job – investigate the company properly before getting involved.

Job offers

Talking of investigating jobs, job offers are another way that many people are getting scammed. There are two main ways that job offers are used as a scam.

1 – They ask for all of your personal information so that they can steal your identity in other ways.

Please do some due diligence with this one by ensuring the company is real. Do a background check them and get as much information as possible. Not just on their own website, but look for reviews elsewhere (LinkedIn, Google etc). Do not just trust their website!

2 – They ask for an advance fee to put you forward for a 100% guaranteed job.

No decent employment agency will ever ask for an advance fee – they make their income from placing great people into great jobs and getting a "finder's fee" of some kind. They would NEVER charge you in advance!

Jesse's notes on investigating

Part of investigating anything, whether it's a company or a product, is reviews. Google has them, Amazon has them, social media has them. The thing with reviews is that it is easy to get someone to write a few good reviews. People also love to just complain. Don't just look at the star rating, read some of the 5 star and the 1 star reviews and find out what is really good or bad about something.

Bad luck stories

This will be an emotional story that is designed to pull on your emotions and make you part with some money.

Don't respond – Even to say no! That will just prove that you're the right type of person for them to target.

If you really want to give money to a deserving place, please do so through a registered charity!

Inheritance Scam

You get a letter saying that someone has left you money in their Will or that there is an inheritance due to you when someone hasn't left a Will. These letters may even use the names of real solicitors, believable email addresses, there may be a website for the company, etc.

If you're in the UK there's an organisation called the Solicitors Regulation Authority (www.sra.org.uk) who you can use to check the authenticity of the letter and the people sending it, if they are solicitors.

However, there are many companies out there who legitimately find people in inheritance cases. A good friend of mine, Kirsty Gray, runs Family Wise Limited and they are one of the leading probate and intestacy companies in the United Kingdom. Their letters have all the hallmarks of authenticity – their Companies House registration number, their Information Commissioner's Office number, their website, telephone number, email, postal address of their office in Wiltshire … what more could you want?

Kirsty's team regularly take calls at their Head Office seeking to find out more information to ensure that the contact is 'above board'/legitimate and they are more than happy to answer any and all questions from callers, about their own letters and those from others as well.

"We would much rather speak to people, allay their concerns and answer their questions so they are happy with the reason we have written, and the process involved, so they understand what is going on. We never ask for any money so any letters from companies asking for money to be transferred should probably go straight in the bin!" Kirsty informed me.

It is always best to check companies out properly and, even if the letter isn't from Family Wise, Kirsty and her team are very happy to provide advice.

Help me to move this cash...... Please!

You might get a letter asking you to help get a large sum of money out of a country, normally from a government official or a solicitor within that country? They may even suggest that it's a bit illegal to move this money? Or that they're trying to get it away from a very bad person?

Look, you know this is wrong, if this was legal they could just move the money using their bank! The truth is that they want it to look slightly illegal so that you never go to the police! NEVER respond! That will just give them the go ahead to keep trying with you.

Top tips for avoiding postal scams

There are a few ways to reduce the amount of risk you are in from postal scams. Firstly, get in touch with the Mailing Preference Service and ask to have your name taken off direct mailing lists in the UK (this won't cover mail that is unaddressed or from other countries).

A no junk mail' sign on your door will stop so much of this stuff getting through to you! At least from your postman!

If you get something you think is a scam, don't respond, and throw it away.

Always background check any company you are giving your details to – if there is an option on any tick box that states you DO NOT want your details given to other companies please tick it!

If you've got something that you're not sure about then show it to someone you trust! If you have someone that might not be as savvy as you, make sure they know that they can come to you for help.

Jesse's thoughts on not responding

Sometimes, whether it is physical mail or email, the people contacting you have your contact details. But very often, scammers are blanket contacting people because they are playing a numbers game. Contacting them does two things. Firstly, it confirms that your contact details are correct. Secondly, it starts a dialogue, which is never a good idea because now they are interested in you. The likelihood is that not many people contact them, so all you are doing is putting out a beacon to say "try to scam me".

I have known people who like to send "f**k off" responses, but all that is doing is alerting them to your presence. The problem with confirming contact details is that they now have valuable contact details that they can sell on the black market – your details are going to be shared with a lot of nasty people. Put the message in the bin, and ignore it!

Phone scams

Phone scams are one of the most common ways for a scammer to try to get to you, your money or even your technology. As I am writing this I can tell you that literally yesterday I had a call from a scammer on my landline phone trying to get me to connect my laptop to his website in the hope that he would gain access to my computer. In this section we are going to cover some of the most common ways for a scammer to use your phone! These are all typically made from cold calls, so let's look at that first.

What is a cold call?

Put very simply it's a company calling you without an appointment trying to sell you something, even if they haven't dealt with you before. They are not necessarily illegal and don't actually count as a scam, but they can be annoying, inconvenient, frustrating, etc and as you will see, there is a reason for being able to manage the calls.

Now this won't block scammers (because they don't care about laws!) but it is worth registering with the TPS (Telephone Preference Service) if these types of calls annoy you! Once on the register it will stop any companies calling you without good reason to do so.

What is illegal is processing your personal data (processing includes storing) without your permission. You will have heard about the General Data Protection Regulation (GDPR), but apart from what you have seen from people who think they know what they are talking about posting on social media, you probably don't know what it's all about. In mentioning this, I can actually see Jesse starting to twitch! This is because he has actually done a lot of work with GDPR, including going through the legal documents (who does that?!) and reading the official guidelines. He has even gained clarification on some of the points in the legal documents from the governing body, the Information Commissioner's Office.

The reality with GDPR and phone calls is that it is a bit complicated, but if you are getting nuisance calls and messages, follow the official complaints guidance.

ico.org.uk/make-a-complaint

Scammers aren't official businesses and don't care about GDPR – so why have we gone into quite so much detail? The problem with businesses processing your data is that so many businesses get hacked. If they are storing your contact details, that's an extra level of risk. It is bad enough that companies that you want to work with have so much of your data, so let's get your data off other company systems. This means that you don't just log a cold call, you should ask them to remove your details from the system.

If you want to really make sure you are in the clear, make sure you write down their company details – get a website and check it while you are on the phone. They should have a way to make a data access request, to see what data of yours that they are holding – and you can request to have it removed. If they are not following your wishes, make a complaint to the ICO.

Mobile phones are getting increasingly clever around alerting you that a phone call is from a potential spam number. Make sure you block these numbers once someone has called you, to make sure that it updates the warning systems.

Common phone scams.

Now, here is the reason I mentioned cold calls above! It can be tough to figure out what is a genuine call and what is a scam. But at least if you are handling cold calls, all you need to manage are the calls from companies that you know (or you might think the call is from them). We talked about this a little in the Your Home "Computer" chapter with the computer repair scam. But there are so many variations, so let's dig deeper.

Bank call

You bank calls saying that there is a problem with your account or your card. For this one they will often sound very professional and they will want you to believe that a fraud of some kind is already taking place on your account and that your money is at risk RIGHT NOW.

They might ask you to go through some security check (trying to get you to give those details freely). They might ask for your account numbers and sort codes etc. They may even blatantly ask for your PIN details. They have even been known to send a courier to collect your debit card associated with this account! They might also advise you to transfer your money to a "safe" account for them to keep hold of the money while they investigate.

THIS SCAM IS MORE COMMON THAN YOU WOULD BELIEVE – please do not agree to any of it. Today I had an issue on one of my credit cards, they called me from a number I didn't recognise and when I said I did not want to go through security checks the lovely lady said "Ok Mr Newton, would you please call us back on the phone number that you trust? I will leave a note on your account explaining why I called you" This in my eyes was the perfect response! And it was so nice to hear!

If you automatically take the stance that you are not happy to give sensitive data out, then it's up to the banks to sort it – and they are becoming more aware and are improving around this.

Jesse's banking experience

I recently had a call from a credit card company. I was immediately wary, even though I was expecting a call from them. They asked me for security information, but never the whole information (i.e. 3rd and 5th character in...) and NEVER the pin. One thing they asked me to provide and I said "NO!". Immediately, they offered me an alternative validation that I was happy with. If I had not been happy with that, there were options.

I was very impressed with the way that they are handling this, in fact that particular supplier has a lot of security that is still easy to use and seem to be getting it right. This isn't just good for my experience, but because it sets a precedent; you are in control and you can be as careful as you need to be.

Compensation calls

"Hello sir! We've been told that you were recently in a car accident that wasn't your fault....... "

You know the call, don't you? Please just don't engage with these calls! They could be genuine companies looking for business, but they could also be scammers. Your best bet here is that you find someone through a recommendation or even through your own insurance company to make sure that you don't get ripped off!

HMRC/Tax man

You might get a recorded message saying that if you don't call back, you're going to be arrested for tax fraud? Or it might be a real person saying that you need to pay X amount on your current tax bill otherwise the police will be sent to you? Maybe they're even offering you a refund because you paid too much tax? Either way, this is complete rubbish! HMRC will not contact you in this way at all. They are trying to use fear as a massive motivator to get either your credit card details or your bank details.

Number spoofing

Please be wary of any call from your bank or credit card company as soon as they say, "well you can see it's us from the number we've called on!"

The technology is now available to "spoof" any phone number the scammer wants to use – so it could look like they are calling from your bank but really, it's a dodgy call centre.

The best thing to do with any call from one of these companies is to explain that you're not happy answering any questions unless you call them back. Then when you do call back please do it from a different phone if you can! The reason for this is that when you hang up on their original call the scammer may not hang up and just waits for you to come back! They then have a fake dialling tone until you've made the call to your bank...

Oh yes, they are sneaky!

Pensions/Investment scams

If you get a call about an unmissable opportunity, please just hang up!
These kinds of things should only be dealt with by people you 100% trust, and definitely NOT someone who has just called you out of the blue!

Anti-scam calls

This could be from a company saying they are a charity helping to support victims of fraud. Or maybe they're calling to renew your TPS membership for an admin fee

(TPS has always been free of charge!) Walk away, hang up, don't even give them space in your head.

The Push Scam

The Push Scam is a particularly horrible scam. It relies on our fear of being defrauded. And the liability is 100% down to you.

There is no comeback, and while your bank will try to help you if this happens the fact is that YOU must have made the transfer, or at very least you gave them access to your bank. There truly is no way of getting this one back from the scammers! It happens like this.

You get a phone call saying that there has been fraudulent activity on your account. After going through a few simple security checks with you (the kind of stuff that I could probably steal quite easily!), they explain that your accounts are on hold for your security and they ask you to go online later and check for any unknown transfers. They explain that they will call you back tomorrow to discuss what to do next.

When you check later you see that a transfer has been made between your own accounts that you didn't do (this bit is important, as transferring between your own accounts is easier to do and doesn't flag up any security warnings).

The next phone call happens and as you've checked your accounts (the main one's name has possibly been changed to "Frozen") and they explain that a new account has been set up for you to transfer your money into.

They give you the account number and sort code to complete the transfer ASAP. Either you do it OR with the extra security details they've now gained from you they do it.

You've just lost all of your money...

The main teachings here are these:

1. Your bank will NEVER ask you to transfer money from your account.
2. Never give ANY security info to someone that calls you! Ask who they are and call them back on a number YOU trust (not the one they've just given you!!)
3. You can stop and take a breather AT ANY TIME! They will try to convince you that this is urgent, must be dealt with NOW etc etc. Your response can easily be this "I completely agree, and I'll call my bank now on a number I trust"
4. Call the bank back from a different phone if you can. (we've explained why earlier!)

What do you do if you get a scam call?

While many of these calls are to random numbers, these guys love to target the elderly. They use fear, manipulation and social engineering techniques to try and get the victim to comply.

DO NOT reveal personal details. No matter who they are they do not need you to tell them any of your personal information. Account number, sort code, PIN details, Mother's maiden name – none of it at all!

Hang up. I know it sounds simple; well, it really is! You have complete control over how much you listen to them. And while I say that I love chatting to them (I want to waste as much of their time as possible!) you don't need to or have to. If they are harassing you or trying to pressure you into something, then just hang up!

Ring the company directly. This is massive in my mind. If you say you're not happy and want to call them back then you can do exactly that! They SHOULD say that you are completely right to do so and the good companies will encourage you to go find the phone number elsewhere from a source you trust (like on the back of your credit card or on your bank statement!). Don't get them to give you a number, it will likely be dodgy.

Don't rush me! If a scammer feels like they're losing, they will always try to put pressure on you. When a person is under pressure, they make silly choices!

Silly things like "we're sending the police round now" or "Your computer has already been hacked" This is exactly the time that you need to stop the call and take a breath.

Staying safe in your home

This book isn't about fear. Well it is a little bit! We want you to be frightened enough to take note and take action. But in reality, we want you to be aware, so that you can be confident in what the risks are and how to handle them. This is like practicing to do an emergency stop – you're not frightened every time you get in the car, but you are ready should something happen.

With that said, hopefully you will now be aware that just being in your own home doesn't mean you are safe from scammers. They are crafty and clever, so you need to be wary.

Chapter 5
Out In The World

Away from the safety of your own home, there is plenty of opportunity for nefarious characters to steal from us. As someone who is very determined to only have nice, helpful people around me. Unfortunately, good natured, helpful people are the most likely to be scammed, because scammers rely on our good human nature to help them. Other than this human nature, the other reason I am fascinated with scams in the real world is that they are generally low tech and essentially magic tricks. Here is one that is like watching something from a movie, because if they are good, it is just like a slick magic trick. Remember, the mark is the person who is being scammed...

Broken vase at a cash machine

This is one of my favourite scams and one done right it's actually a thing of beauty. It takes a couple of players or fraudsters and it takes one mark - lets set the scene.

You, the mark, go up to a cash machine/ATM (whatever you prefer to call it). Having put your card in the machine, you enter your PIN number in and tell it you want cash.

Somebody near you drops a vase or a glass thing it sounds expensive, you look and check they're okay, you see that other people are looking after them. You turn back to the machine and your transaction and you take your card. You take the cash out and you put your card in your wallet. You put the cash in your wallet you carry on with your merry day.

When you go and put your card into the machine there is someone over your shoulder looking at the card you're using. If they have a similar card to you in their possession then it's game on, and after a nod, everyone involved knows its action stations.

That Scammer also watches over your shoulder to get your pin number. If you don't believe this is possible, trust me; I've done it more than 100 times just to prove to people it's possible. Some of those people aren't very happy with me, but it gets the point across! If he gets the PIN number, he gives a nod to their friendly person, who is a young lady holding a vase in a bag.

She then waits for the magical moment when your card starts coming out of the machine. When it starts coming out, she drops the vase and CRASH! You, as a normal human being, turn to look.

In the second or two that you have used to look, the scammer who was looking over your right shoulder leans over you, swipes the card and swaps it for the card that you had that looks very similar.

When you turn back to the card machine you take your card out and put it in your wallet. I would like to bet that you don't check that it's actually your name on the card as long as it looks the same. If you are even slightly concerned that you have been distracted, you are probably more relieved that the cash is there - you then take your cash, put it in your wallet and are as happy as anything. Now the fraudsters now have your card and your PIN number, and you don't even think anything is wrong.

If you've just taken a load of cash out there's normally a reason for it, so be honest with yourself, how often do you check your bank statement and how often do you look at the cards in your wallet to make sure they're still your ones?

I've been delivering talks around the UK for the last six months on this subject and the average time for people in those rooms to check their statements is once in every three or four days so let's say it's every four days. The average amount that you can take your own cash in the different bank accounts I've had in those rooms it ranges from £250 up to £1000 per day so will go somewhere in the middle and say it's £500 per day as an average.

So, if I've got four days to take out £500 a time that means I can get £2000 out of your card before you even notice I'm doing it. Talking of cards, here is something a little newer…

Contactless technology

Now, my credit card and my bankcard have contactless technology. It has a little funny symbol on it to let you know. If you're paying for something under £30 you don't even have to put in and use your PIN. This technology is brilliant because it means that you don't show scammers or fraudsters your pin number every time you go to a card machine but there are some down sides, the big one is that it means your cards are always open to being copied by someone. It's really not that hard to go and buy enough kit from technology websites that to make a small machine which constantly looks for card details.

And what details can I pick up?

They can get your 16-digit card number, your starting date, your expiry date and basically everything I need to spend money with your card online. The one thing they cannot get is your PIN; but think about when you're buying something online - you don't enter your PIN! You enter the details that I can never steal from you using that contactless technology!

How can we beat this one?

"It must be really expensive and difficult to solve!" I hear you shout!

It's actually ridiculously simple. Many wallets, phone cases with card holders and other card holders have RFID protection, which will stop readers from picking up the card details. The only issue is that this is NOT a standard, and you typically have to go out of your way to buy something to suit. Most people are quite fussy over their wallet, phone case and bags – firstly from an aesthetic perspective and secondly from a functionality point of view. This means that having in-built RFID capability is not exactly a priority and if that was what I was trying to achieve, we would make very little difference.

However, there is another option – RFID blocker cards! These look a bit like a credit card, as they are designed to go into a card slot in your phone or wallet. They are also relatively cheap; especially as I know that it once saved me £4000.00 when walking through a London market... (but that is a story for another day!). Shameless plug number two is that you can buy them from https://www.mentaltheft.co.uk/shop

If the only thing you learned from reading this whole book is to buy yourself an RFID blocker, please go and do it!

PIN Keypads

I'm not sure where you're based. I'm not sure if you know what Tesco is. It's a massively successful supermarket in the UK (others are available!), if you're based in the US then think of Walmart? I'm now fully expecting loads of tweets explaining the difference between Tesco and Walmart so let's just go with this.

It's a big shop.

Ok?

Here's my story.

I was in Tesco picking up a few bits, as my wife had messaged me and asked me to get them on the way home. Having picked up everything I was asked to get (trying to get some good husband points so I can play on the Xbox later) and I walked to the till. I stand behind this lovely old lady and we start chatting. She's telling me all about how her son, his wife and her grandchild are heading down to see her for the weekend. She's excited about taking her grandson out crabbing (if you haven't been, try it!) because we live on the south coast and her grandson loves going.

Her shopping has been packed by the lady behind the counter – the amount was £34 and something pence, the £34 bit has stuck in my head because it's just over the contactless amount and therefore this lady would not be able to use contactless payment.

"Cash or card" the till lady said.

"Oh, I'll pay by card please" said my new friend.

The lady behind the till then handed over the card machine and the card went into the slot. My friend then proceeded to show me her PIN as she was tapping it in.

She's literally just met me, but there she was blatant as anything just showing me her pin number! I swear she even lent in a bit closer to me to make sure I had a good view of what she typed!

But it isn't just unsuspecting pensioners... Having spent a morning using magic to steal PINs at a corporate event, I sat in a service station with a cup of tea, having a break from driving across the country. Whilst sat there, I had a perfect view of the touch screen machines that a certain fast-food restaurant now uses to take orders. When the order is complete you can use your contactless to pay if it is under £30, but if it's over then I get a great view of your PIN. And you also show me exactly where you put that card away too. I don't even need to be a MentalTheft expert, I just needed eyes!

One of my friends is one of the best pickpockets I have ever seen. I've seen him take wallets from pockets, phones from jackets, watches from wrists and even a belt from a guy's trousers. Without the victim even noticing. One time he took a wallet, took two cards from it and then put the wallet back. All whilst telling me exactly what he was doing without the victim noticing a thing!

The point here is that it really isn't that difficult to take a wallet off someone. You wouldn't know until I was long gone. If you have shown me your PIN, I can tell you now that I will be spending that money VERY quickly. If it is a credit card, there is some level of protection, and almost none on a debit card. But increasingly, banks are not compensating people when a card is used with the correct PIN.

The Train Steal

I was heading home the other day after delivering work in central London. I was settling down on the train and it was a nice enough journey, with my phone out and watching Netflix.

It was a quiet train, just me and a guy in front who is blatantly making a purchase over the phone. Now, my ears prick up when I hear certain things, and the magic words I heard which made me start listening?

"Yes, I'll have that one please how quickly can you deliver?"

This is the kind of thing that a scammer would listen out for, and as soon as I heard those words, I got my pen out. I already had a notepad out because I jot down ideas as and when I have them and I'll have a look through them on the train. Before you say, I watch Netflix on my phone, so I like a separate pad!

I started making notes.

He then proceeded to say out loud his full address, he then gave me his 16 digit card number, he then told me the start and expiry date for his credit card. He then turned the card over and gave me the three digits on the back.

What else do I need to make a purchase on this guy's account?

I could go online and buy stuff that's easy to sell on, and as it cost me nothing, I'd get it gone quickly at a reduced price so that I don't have to worry about dodgy goods.

Back to my man on the train - I didn't really want to go and talk to him.

I've had situations before when I've tried to advise people on security issues and they almost get confrontational, and very, very defensive.

Here's what I did.

I left the train before him so I took my notepad I had all of his details and underneath all of his details I wrote a little message just saying thank you very much for your card details and your address details, maybe I should go and buy myself a little present?

As I was walking past him, I handed him the note and just said "oh I think this is yours".

And I'm off.

As the train departed, I looked at him and I could see he was reading the note and his jaw dropped.

He looks scared.

I really, really hope that you learn a lesson and you don't go telling people your credit card details in a public place.

And if you're that guy that was on that train, I am sorry, but I hope it worked!

Wrapping Service

This is an oldie but a goodie. This normally happens around Christmas time when people are buying presents for their loved ones. We love our families, and we are buying loads of stuff to try and make other people smile.

If you go to some big shopping centres, there will sometimes be a stand offering to wrap your presents for you, there might be a small charge or there might be a give a donation to this charity kind of charge, but it won't be much.

It's normally very professionally done they've got some examples of presents they've already wrapped for people and the people behind the counter look lovely.

As all scammers and fraudsters normally do. The thing is, if they are nice and professional looking, no-one will question it, not even the shopping centre. They have enough to deal with during Christmas shopping season.

You leave five presents with them to be wrapped up and they agree that you can come back in two hours; you even get your ticket that proves which presents are yours.

You go away, you have a nice cup of coffee or maybe a cup of tea? Maybe even a Danish - you're allowed it's Christmas! You're happy in the fact that someone else is doing the wrapping AND you're giving back to charity!

You come back and pick up your parcels, you find everything wrapped beautifully and you take them away with you. You put them underneath your Christmas tree at home and look forward to the big day.

On Christmas Day your loved ones are opening their presents they find the box for the right thing but it's now full of bricks or just some weights.

That made it feel like it was the right weight!

What they actually did to you was they switched out your present for something that was absolutely worthless, and they can now go and sell your present to the highest bidder.

Now, I think all of these scams are horrible but this one just gets my back up a little bit more because it messes up Christmas for you and your family. Wrap your presents up yourself – or pay someone you actually know to do them.

The Vase Drop

Don't worry, I haven't copied and pasted a story – this is a different way of stealing something using a vase – who knew that scammers like vases so much?!

Any good person who has bumped into a stranger and broke an expensive possession would offer to pay them for it. People tend to feel responsible when they break things, and that's what vase drop scammers are counting on.

The traditional name for this scam, melon drop scamming, gets its name from cons who originally used melons at a time when melon prices were at a record high in Japan. The cons would bump into Japanese tourists, drop melons, and demand payment. The tourists would pay jacked-up prices without question.

The modern version of this scam involves throwing worthless broken glass in a box and wrapping it up to look nice. The scammers scan the crowd for someone who isn't paying attention and bump into them, making it seem as if it was the mark's fault. They then explain that the box contained an expensive vase — usually a gift for their mother, boss's wife, dying grandma, anyone — which is now broken. They may even produce a receipt to prove its value. You're lucky if you're out less than £100 after this scam.

The Pigeon Drop

The pigeon drop is simple, complicated, illogical, and makes perfect sense all at the same time. In one variation, a person approaches to tell you they found money and don't know what to do with it. As you discuss the possibilities, they hint at splitting the profit with you. You are giving them advice, after all.

Eventually, the con will seek counsel from an authority figure, who will advise allowing time for someone to claim the cash. Until then, one person, an attorney, or a joint account can hold the cash. Swindlers then convince you to put up cash as a good faith deposit for the larger sum later. With visions of shopping sprees and paid-off bills, you comply.

In a more dramatic variation shown in the movie The Sting, a scammer poses as an injured person who needs to get a large sum of cash somewhere quickly. Another person assists them along with you, but they can't run the errand. The poor victim begs you to make the delivery. As a sign of good faith, you leave something valuable with them, and the helper demonstrates the best way to conceal the money using your money. Afterward, you scurry off to deliver the cash, but once you unwrap the package, you discover only bits of paper. If a stranger offering you large amounts of cash sounds too good to be true, it probably is.

The Ring Reward

A damsel in distress is always a good way to start a scam – it appeals to our human nature. And when a very pretty girl pretends to have lost her engagement ring, even the toughest alpha males let their guards down. She asks you if you've found a ring and then leaves her info, promising a decent reward for its return. A short time later, some lucky stiff approaches you, having "found" the ring. The cons are counting on you to offer money for the ring either to secure the larger reward or out of the goodness of your heart.

Whether you're cold-hearted or good-natured, any attempt to secure that ring will leave your pockets lighter – those contact details are not real and there is no reward. Scammers using rings for this con or variations of it have a stack of cheap costume rings at the ready. They can sell you jewellery all day, so inspect any found rings carefully and don't give any money out.

The Lottery Ticket Scam

In the lottery ticket scam, con artists convince their intended victim to buy a worthless piece of paper. Before the popularity of cell phones, cons provided forged newspapers as proof of the winning numbers, but these days, a fake hotline or website is used to seal the deal. This con requires masterful story-spinning and an inside man who befriends the mark.

One scammer reveals that they've won a lottery prize, but he can't claim the cash because he owes money to the government, who will confiscate the winnings. In the original version of the scam, the winners are scared illegal immigrants without ID or legal papers. They're afraid that when they claim the prize, they'll be deported. The con will ask for opinions and help, then they have the victim call a hotline to verify the numbers.

Once the story is spun, the con offers to sell the ticket at a discount. The inside man convinces the victim to buy the ticket. Unfortunately, when they try to claim their winnings, they find out that the only winner was the con artist.

Remember, if there is something against the law involved, it's probably worse than you think!

The Bank Examiner

Of course, you'd never let just anyone examine your bank account, and hustlers know this. That's why they figure out crafty ways to do it. They rope you into this con by posing as investigators and asking for your help.

In this con, scammers convince helpful bank patrons to withdraw money and hand it over to be examined under the guise of matching serial numbers, marking bills, or auditing a teller. They then use sleight of hand to switch real cash for bogus bills or simply walk off on "official" business. Variations of this scam include claiming a teller is suspected of passing counterfeit bills and they need to examine your money for the operation.

To prevent becoming a victim of this scam, refuse to cooperate with any bank examiners that come calling. If you want to help catch a thief or sort out your account, go into your bank and speak with a real service representative. Remember what we said about doorstep scams and checking with the authorities that they are who they say? This still applies here.

The Overpayment Scam

The overpayment scam evolved from several old and still active forms of bank fraud. It allows con artists to write bad cheques, skate off with the goods, and even get cash back. The main forms these frauds take is counterfeiting, paper-hanging, and cheque-kiting. Counterfeiters forge cheques, paper-hangers pay with cheques written on closed accounts, and cheque-kiters write bad cheques and get cash back to cover a previous bad cheque. In all cases, the cheques eventually bounce. These schemes mostly affect banks and businesses, but the popularity of online shopping has opened up new opportunities for scammers. Now, the counterfeit or paper-hang cheques are used as payment and leave you with the bill.

These are the cons that made Frank Abagnale Jr. more than $2 million in the '60s – he's the guy that Leonardo DiCaprio played in *Catch Me If You Can*. Anyone looking for work, selling on an auction site, renting property, or selling a car is a target. The scammer sends a counterfeit cheque for more than the settled amount, and when the honest seller or contractor discovers the "mistake," they alert the scammer. The seller is instructed to deposit the cheque and then transfer the difference back to the buyer.

Most people assume that their bank would catch a fake cheque on sight, but several days can pass before the bank realizes that they've been had. In the meantime, banking regulations require funds to be available the next day. This loophole makes the scam possible, leaving the account owner liable for cheques they deposit. To avoid this scam, never transfer funds to a stranger or accept cheques for more than the agreed amount. If you have to deposit a cheque, wait more than a few days to let the cheque clear and ask your bank when it has FULLY cleared their system.

Jesse's Thoughts on Cheques

Checks or cheques, what are they grandad? I'm being facetious, but we get a lot of people that are very afraid of new technology – you will have read the chapter on passwords with the biometrics and password checkers.

But in fact, old technology is far more dangerous. No matter what technology or period we are talking about, there is a constant cycle of improvement for technologies as frauds happen and the technology is updated to counteract it. Look at all of the things they do to notes to stop people making fake money. But as a technology is slowly replaced, all of the work goes on the new technology. This means that updates to both the old technology and the processes associated with it are not improved, giving scammers plenty of time to work out ways of breaking that system.

Many banks and businesses refuse cheques nowadays, so there is no reason for you to do any different.

The Mustard Dip

In this scam, a helpful stranger tells you that you've got something on your coat and offers to wipe it off for you. Before you know it, they're removing your jacket. That helpful stranger is also removing your wallet and any other expensive possessions in your coat or pockets. You've just become a victim of the mustard dip, aka the mustard squirter, named for the technique of squirting mustard on the victim's coat to make the con believable.

Most cons rely on distraction, shame, and confusion, and in the case of the mustard dip, confusion is key. While the victim tries to figure out how they got mustard on their coat, their guard is down, and that's exactly where scammers want it. If a stranger points out some gooey substance on your clothes, thank them, decline their help, and clean it yourself.

The Flop

The original version of this con required a brave hustler, usually with an old injury, who would step in a car's path and flop onto the hood. They would then either demand compensation immediately or go to the hospital. An examination would reveal the old injury, and the insurance company paid out.

The modern version nets less money but is safer for the hustler. After the flop, they insist that they feel fine and don't need medical attention, but their computer, iPad, or other expensive item is broken. You're just glad they aren't hurt or talking about suing you, so you give them some money to replace it. If you're reluctant to do so, a helpful stranger or angry witness might pull you aside to convince you.

Of course, that "helpful stranger" is a friend of the con artist, who threw an item that was already broken against your bumper and quickly positioned themselves in front of it. The only feasible way to get out of this scam is to insist on calling the emergency services to report the accident and avoid future legal trouble.

The scammer will probably make up an excuse and leave.

Chapter 6
In The Office

Being in the office means that we are exposed to the outside world and this has a lot of implications. Anything that was true with your home security and personal IT is true in your work environment. The difference is that scammers are increasingly going for businesses because they often have the cash and the need to save face that makes them an ideal target.

If you think it is embarrassing for an individual to be scammed, it is even more embarrassing for a business who has a responsibility to its staff and its clients. This means that they are more likely to pay scammers large sums of money to make the problem go away. This is especially true when you have things such as GDPR to consider. Businesses have a duty to inform customers of data breaches, so this is pretty serious.

Even more so, there are a lot of people in a business, and as we have discussed already, people are the weakest link in any security system. This means there are as many potential weak points as there are staff in any business. As a staff member, you need to hold yourself responsible for keeping yourself and, to the best of your ability, the company safe. We will discuss the responsibility of the business in keeping you safe in the next chapter, however, irrespective of who anyone sees as being at fault, there have been enough examples of scams crippling businesses to take note. This could be your job and the jobs of your colleagues at risk.

It sounds pretty sensationalist, but the reality is that it is fairly regular to hear of businesses paying millions of dollars to hackers, and those are just the ones we know about.

So, what can you do about it?

As per everything that we teach, the first step is being aware and being wary. Once you have this, sometimes it's solvable by a fairly easy solution.

Gone Phishing Again

Phishing emails are the downfall of many businesses, yet one of the easiest things to fall for. I know what you are thinking, I have already read about phishing in this book, are you running out of material?

If we had written this book a few years ago, we would have just had one big section in the "Your Home Computer" chapter. However, these days phishing is such a big problem for businesses, that we really had to address it as a separate issue.

OK, so I talked about being sensationalist, Hiscox Insurance state that in 2020 a small UK business is SUCCESSFULLY hacked every 19 seconds. That's pretty sensational. I'm not fear mongering to sell newspapers here, this is a genuine problem. Around half of cyber-attacks in the UK are caused by phishing emails.

With well over half of emails being spam, it's really hard to tell what is real and what isn't any more. It is even worse in a business environment; you should be getting the following question a lot.

"Is this email from a company I never heard of a new customer/supplier, or just a scammer trying to gain access to our systems?"

If you are not even seeing suspect scam emails, it's not because you are not getting them, it's because you are not aware.

The other problem with work emails is that different email addresses are used from around the company for different platforms – marketing teams might be using Canva, Hootsuite, Mailchimp, multiple social media platforms and a whole load of other software. Management are probably signed up to a lot of different business magazines. Operations often use online planning tools. If any one of these tools or subscriptions gets hacked, you are at risk. Especially with anything that has the same email address and password!

There are lots of reasons why this is relevant, but the most important one is that no-one sees these apps as a security risk. If you get an email from a bank, you are probably pretty wary (especially after reading this book!). But do you care about your marketing platforms? If an email that looks like one of those comes through, takes you to a realistic looking site and asks you to sign in… but really, it's a scammer taking your details. How much damage can they do with the details you gave on sign in?!

The trouble is that without you even knowing, any click on a link by a dodgy email can be downloading some bit of software that is quietly letting a hacker gain access to your company, and then the trouble starts. The key is to look out for scam emails and delete them as soon as possible – DO NOT CLICK!

Jesse's Tips To Spot Scam emails

As you start looking out for them, you will start getting really good at spotting the signs for dodgy emails. Here is a quick guide:

- The "To" and "From" email addresses don't look real (check the spelling), or are blank
- Security issue emails don't normally have links
- Hover over click here links to see where they send you – if it looks weird, don't click on it
- Often scam emails have terrible spelling and grammar mistakes, including simple words missing
- Do you even have an account with the company? Remember, they are just guessing, so will often try from companies you don't deal with.

Remember, if you are unsure about an email, even hitting unsubscribe is risky. If it is not a legitimate company, it is better to mark it as spam, or even set up rules to automatically delete them. If you have an IT department, report it to them and they may even set up a group policy to protect everyone.

Message from the Boss

Remember the three types of Mental Theft? If phishing emails come under placement, then this next way of scamming people comes under belief. It is a lot more effort and a lot more audacious, but I can tell you that it is happening more often and is extremely lucrative. It relies on a very simple idea – if you get a message from your boss to do something, you will probably do as you are told without questioning it – especially if the instruction is part of your standard job role. So, let's have a look at a real-world example of this actually happening.

A good friend of mine, Matthew Ruddle, recently started working with a local Chamber of Commerce.

He was really excited about it all and having just started his new business he thought this was a great way to give back to his local community.

He had been in the position for roughly a week when he got an email from the big boss asking him to complete some urgent work. They needed some gifts sent out to suppliers that had really helped them out this year. It wasn't going to be a massive amount considering their budget or considering the amount they spent with these companies but keeping these suppliers on side was worth a small fortune to the chamber.

Matt said he was sure he could help and asked her to send over the information and let him know what was needed.

The response was pretty quick.

> *"I need 4 lot of £200 voucher from Amazon, can you purchase please, scratch off codes on back and email over me.*
>
> *Am heading in to a meeting now but this needs to be done within hour."*

The email seemed quite abrupt and wasn't anything like the kind of work that Matt had been told he would be carrying out. He didn't have access to any of the group's funding so this would have to be paid from his own personal money and claimed back later on.

But something did not seem right.

The signature was good, saying the right name and their correct position.

But some of the wording was off. There were words missing? And silly things like the s missing off "lots" which just wasn't right for the person that Matt knew!

He backed off. He didn't get the vouchers. And I'm so glad he didn't!

After a bit of digging, he realised the email address wasn't quite right either, it was close but not right.

He contacted the person involved and they had no idea what he was talking about. He then did the best thing possible and got the I.T. team involved too.

They did all they could to ensure their network wasn't hacked (it wasn't) but this was quite a good targeted attack.

They knew Matthew's name and email address. They knew his bosses email address and they knew each of their positions. They tried to use this against Matt. They may have found out about his recent new position from a press release in the local news? And if he had sent the vouchers? It would have been 100% his fault.

Well done Matt! Good job!

Thank you to Matt for sharing the story. Now the details on this are a little sketchy – Mostly because when Matt and I went through it all I was actually on a school run, but that's not the point! I have heard many different versions of these attacks and they're getting more and more regular.

I've heard of one example where the MD of a company asked an accounts assistant to transfer payment to a new supplier asap and he couldn't do it because he was jumping on a plane at that precise moment.

The MD supplied full bank details of the new supplier but couldn't do it himself at all. Weird huh? Thankfully on this occasion the person they had targeted was not yet allowed to authorise payments, and when she took it higher up the chain it was stopped from even entering the system.

In the case of either of these stories, once the money or vouchers are gone, there is very little that can be done about it. A few hundred pounds of vouchers might not seem like a lot, but with setting up suppliers (vendors) with the ability to transfer large sums of money unnoticed, this is quite a big risk.

Important Considerations

There are a lot of lessons to be learnt here.

1. It is not that difficult to get very specific information about people, from social media, websites, press releases, phishing attacks, hacks etc.
2. No one honest will mind their payment going through a security check, and they don't normally take long enough to cause delay.
3. No boss should mind you calling them to make sure the email is really from them.
4. No scammer will get away with this if we always remember to verify the information that is put in front of us.

Why low tech is the new high-tech

I get asked a lot how my skills can help in the high-tech arena of Cyber Theft and the answer is simple. I don't attack your technology; I won't even try! I attack the human side of technology.

Think about it, if I can get the username and password details of one of your employees then how much damage can I do within your systems before you even know I'm there?

Even worse than that; I may not do any damage at all, I may just lurk in your system stealing all the information I can get my hands on and the only thing that will stop me is that user changing their password! To be honest, I would normally have access to more than one person's details anyway, so even if my first victim changes their details I'll have access through victim 2, 3 and 4 anyway!

I read somewhere recently that one of the big banks did a study on "over the shoulder" hacks – these are the times when you sit on the train and log in to your computer and I'm literally sat in the seat behind you writing down the details you use – the study says that over 91% of these types of hacks are successful.

I'll say that again.

OVER 91%!

I have no idea how they got to that number, because there must be so many unknowns, such as times when it wasn't even detected. When is the last time you checked if your loving staff were safe with typing in their email addresses, usernames and passwords details? Also how often do they change them? Are they working on the train or other public transport?

It's a scary tactic and as humans we're far too trusting that the stranger behind us is a friend, or at least not an enemy. But it's not just travelling where trust is causing problems, what about at your own site?

Delivery note

A delivery biker goes into a company reception with a delivery for Mrs. Smithe. The receptionist replies "I'm sorry we don't have a Mrs. Smithe here."

Biker "This is company X isn't it?"

Receptionist "Yes."

Biker "And you're sure there's no Mrs. Smithe? I know I need to get a signature from her for it so I'm guessing it's valuable."

Receptionist "I'm sorry but no there's no Mrs. Smithe here."

Biker "Ok I'll give the office a call and try to figure this out."

The Biker then takes out his mobile phone and notices it has no battery.

Biker "I'm really sorry, any chance I could use your phone to call the office? My battery has died! I love technology but hate when it lets me down!"

The nice receptionist let's him use the phone and the call blatantly proves to the biker that he's in the wrong place. It's a mix up at the sender's end.

Biker "I'm so sorry about that, thank you so much for your help!"

Delivery Biker leaves the office with a cheery wave.

What he's actually just done is dial a premium rate number that he owns which is charging £XX per minute. I've heard of some very skilled people who have managed to make 5 calls at once, used the hold option on the phone system so each call stays active and pays him 5 times the amount!

This is just one example, but all of these sorts of scams have a common theme. We are taught to be friendly and helpful. It really goes against our nature to be anything other than that, especially in front facing roles. But we need to make sure that we have guidelines that we are working to – being wary of people and make sure that you are the one in control of any situation.

Chapter 7
As A Business Owner

Cyber security – it's not what you got into business for, and frankly it's a load of nonsense that you don't understand. You probably don't have a strategy other than having some passwords to log in. My job in this chapter is to make you start to care, and then help you do something about it!

If you are sat there thinking, "I've got an IT person", or even "I've got an IT department", and think that means you've got it covered, you're probably wrong.

That is absolutely not the fault of your IT staff either – it is your lack of understanding. You wouldn't expect a sales director to do the accounts. They both use computers too! The reality is that as an owner of a business, you need to have a handle on the cyber security strategy, just like you should have an understanding on unlocking and locking the office.

It is also important to instil in every person in an office that they are "responsible" for the security of a business and making people aware of the possible dangers is a key part of this. Depending on the business will depend on how much they hold people responsible. In our experience, the level of training and protection in place means that although an individual may have been the bit that broke in the system (or lack there-of), not enough has been done by any company to actually hold them accountable. As a business, it is your responsibility to put the systems in place to protect your staff, and also to protect the business from the staff's human nature.

In the last chapter we talked about the delivery note – in that story, the receptionist that you hired because they were friendly, approachable and helpful was preyed upon. It is not their fault; they are just being who you wanted them to be! You need to look at how your systems and processes are set up to make sure that she, and any other member of staff, is as secure as they can possibly be!

The stats on cybersecurity vary depending on the source – but it's fair to say that it is likely that you will get a breach at some level over the next few years. Your business is already receiving phishing emails regularly, probably daily, and every single one is a risk to your business. Consider what the worst that could happen would be. If you aren't sure, it is something like this:

- You get hacked and locked out of all of your software systems, stopping your company from operating
- As part of being locked out, you no-longer have access to any of your data
- You have to pay millions of pounds/dollars to get access to any of the systems and data
- Your company must, by law, contact all the people who have data in that system to notify them of a breach
- There is a possibility that the hacker sells all of the data taken from your systems (contact details, bank details, card details etc) on the dark web
- After paying the ransom, the hacker still doesn't give you back control of your systems.

Could your business even survive this? Because it is happening all the time. Even if the ransom is a lot less, £30k or £100k would be extremely impactful on your business, let alone the potential effect on reputation.

The same principals of protecting yourself with password checkers and being wary about phishing emails all apply, but now you have a lot of people who fall under your responsibility. Even more so, they are all a potential risk to the business, and you cannot assume that they think the same way that you do. In fact, neither of you think like a criminal, just by the nature of your job roles, which is why this book is here to help!

It's the simple things

Remember when I told you that criminals like to go for the easiest targets? Just like with phishing emails, it's something as simple as a click on an email that can take down a business. But people like me like the quick and quiet wins, because you can syphon off a bit of money at a time without people noticing. Without the press, we can fly in under the radar and make a tonne of money without anyone really trying to catch us. Do you remember the WannaCry ransomware attack on the NHS?

The truth is that the people who caused that made very little money, because as soon as the ransom was put into a bank, the whole world was watching and waiting for someone to cash out. Considering it was a global attack and affected a lot of people, I have seen estimates of maybe a couple of hundred thousand dollars, and with the risk of the world's security forces descending on them. That said, the damage was huge, with the cost to the National Health Service (NHS) estimated in the region of £92million.

How do you make the simple steal?

It is worth pointing out that when I talk about the fact that I like to fly under the radar, this isn't because I am an actual criminal – I just know how to be one. That skillset is why I get invited to test security for a wide range of businesses. With all of the public speaking I do, I normally scare people by stealing their PIN enough that they start to consider the possibilities for their organisation, and I am often the answer to the ensuing questions.

A little while ago I was invited into an office to evaluate how good they were at security. I was invited into the MD's office where I met himself and his chief of security. It seemed a bit weird at first because when they asked me to come in, they told me that I would never be able to beat their security because it was completely secure. Anyone with a bit of sense knows that no system is completely protected, and I quite like a challenge, so I decided to go along.

Whilst enjoying a lovely cup of tea and they explained to me that they had the top-notch security systems with infallible email security and the firewall was amazing. There was no way I would ever get into their systems.

I asked them why they actually invited me in the first place if they thought their security was so good, and the MD said to me "Well you never really know do you?" I distinctly felt like the MD didn't really believe I could do it, but the chief of security didn't believe in infallible.

They didn't immediately get me to try to break into their systems, which is handy because I am no computer hacker, which is why I normally insist on working to my own timescale. Instead, they showed me the computer systems, walked me around the building, from the offices to the reception area. It was like a statement of pride as they showed me every area of the business having paid a lot of money to improve their security. In fairness, it actually looked pretty good.

As they took me round, they introduced me to lots of the staff, a really nice company with a lot of lovely staff. Everyone was pleasantly getting on with their work.

We eventually get back to the MD's office at which point they mentioned that I haven't even talked about my fees yet. I explained to them that if I couldn't break into their systems at all then there would be no fee however if I could break into their systems, I asked how much that would be worth to them.

The chief of security started looking worried. The MD started to look even more confident, this was going to be a very cheap consultancy for him!

"OK, I said, "what about this? how much do you have in your business bank account right now?"

He looked a bit puzzled and said I would expect it's about £2,000,000.

"So, if I could hack into your accounts package and send myself a payment that means I could pay myself £2,000,000 without it bouncing, without it being stopped. But let's be honest if I did that, you'd notice it far too easily so how about if I just went for 1% of what's in your bank account? A nice easy 20,000 pounds."

The MD laughed: "Obviously you'll never be able to do that. So yes, that would be fair."

"Great. Would you mind logging out of your computer and letting me borrow it?" I said.

The MD did so.

I walked over to his desk sat down at his computer. I immediately logged into his computer, opened up the accounts package on the system, logged into that and set myself up as a new supplier.

I then created an invoice against my account to the tune of £20,000 for services rendered.

At this point, about 3 minutes later, I looked up from the screen to see the two gentlemen looking very comfortable, expecting to be sat there for quite some time. The MD was probably only sat there because he still had half a coffee left.

I caught his eye, so beckoned them both over to look at the screen.

On the screen they could see the invoice with a dialogue box to post the invoice.

As their jaws hit the floor, I asked "Shall I hit enter now?"

I didn't charge them £20,000.

I actually charged them a lot less than that and told them how I did it.

While I was on the tour of the office, I had my phone in my hand and I switched it to video recorder. This meant I was recording everything that I pointed my phone at, just with a simple click to start and stop recording. Whilst on the tour, I had seen five different sticky notes with the usernames and passwords attached to computer monitors. I was particularly interested when I went into the accounts department and saw a sticky note on the monitor of the financial director!

Now admittedly I needed access to the building to see most of this information. If I hadn't had access to the building, I probably wouldn't have seen four of the notes.

But the financial director had his own office with nice big windows and his back to the car park. So, to see his username and password you wouldn't even need to be in the building, you could have walked past and just taken a photo of it.

Jesse's all-seeing eye

Paul has an old phone, which is why he thinks you have to walk up to a building to take a photo through a window! The FD, with his back to the car park, was at risk from someone in a car with a decent camera, or possibly with one of the very impressive new releases of mobile phones. In fact, if they had been above ground level, a zoom lens from another building would have been enough. And you have no control over other companies and their security.

While everyone likes to think that hackers are hidden in their dark basements with a shed load of computers around them, the truth is that a lot of the time they're dressed like the average person and they're walking past your window.

Please don't make it easy for them.

Is it you or your staff?

In my years of dealing with business security, it has become extremely clear that the best form of attack is to utilise human nature. This is why I said earlier that whilst your staff may be the cause of a breach, they generally can't, or at least shouldn't, be held accountable for it. This next example really illustrates this.

Modus Operandi

A while ago I was asked to look at a secure compound for vans. I thought, this is a two-man job, and so easily employed the help of a good friend.

It was a large building, very grey concrete, a security hut at the front and the outside had the typical wire metal fencing all around it.

You can easily look around the building whilst walking around the outside of the fence and you could spot if any windows or doors were open without getting access to the compound itself.

We went at night-time to have a snoop around without being spotted. It's pretty simple to stake out a building without attracting attention. We just pulled up in a car, had a look from outside for 10 to 15 minutes, then moved the car to a different position and had a look from the new position. No-one ever bats an eyelid.

The front of the compound had a driveway entrance with one of those barriers that lift out of the ground, so that they could stop vehicles coming through. Right next to it was a hut so that the security guard could sit sheltered. The guard that was on duty was blatantly on his own and had a little television that we believe was cycling through video feeds from security cameras around the site.

Across the road from the hut was a nice parking area with one of those food vans locked up – it was too late to be serving food on the estate. It was a really nice vantage point to watch the front of this compound without anyone noticing.

We sat in this position for about 2 hours, literally just trying to get an idea of what went on at the site. We noticed that every 30 minutes the security guard would leave the hut and go for a walk. He would always go in the same direction whenever he left and was regular as clockwork. He would return almost exactly 10 minutes later, every time.

On the guard's fourth trip, we decided to confirm what was on the TV screen. Whilst I kept watch, he waited about 30 seconds for the guard to leave and then he ran over to the hut. It was indeed a security camera feed, showing us exactly where the cameras were watching. He took a quick photo of it to make sure we knew where they were hitting and so that if we did break in any point, we would know where the risk areas were, and where the blind spots would be.

Having seen everything that he needed, he ran back to me and we started coming up with a plan. We decided that we were going to try and break into the building that night in case we got a different security guard, who may have a different routine. When he went on his next walk, we walked past the hut and turned to the left of the building; the opposite direction that the guard left and returned to the hut.

When we first looked around the outside of the compound, we had seen that there was a door that seemed to be ajar, near where lots of vans were parked up. We made a direct line for that door, which turned out to be a fire escape. Sure enough, it was ajar, and we prised it open with the tips of our fingers. Wedging a block of wood to keep the door open, we could now come and go as we pleased without having to worry about locks or alarms.

Once inside, we barely even went two metres before seeing a box on the wall. It was one of those boxes that people keep keys in. The keys to every van parked outside the building were there for the taking. Helpfully, they had even been as nice as to make sure they were marked up with the number plates of the vans, so we wouldn't have to try keys in locks.

We grabbed a key each and slipped out of the building with plenty of time for the guard to come back.

On his next walk, we waited for the guard to head off out of immediate earshot.

Jumping into our vehicles, we were absolutely shocked at what we saw! Both vehicles were full of products and boxes; we didn't know what they were, but we realised we were no longer just stealing vans, we were stealing their customer's products as well!

Off we go.

This is not like a Hollywood film, when the thief wheelspins the stolen vehicles away from the scene! We drive out carefully. Trying to drive like a courier would (and no, I do not mean wheel spinning away from the scene!!!).

We drive to just around the estate and park the vans up. We lock them and leave them in a well-lit area in front of a building with security cameras pointing to the front - we really don't want anything stolen from them after we've done this!

And we make a call to the head of security for our client.

Me: "You know we were planning on a recce of the depots and hoping to make a break in this week? "

Him: "Yes?"

Me: "We've done it."

Him: "The recce?"

Me: "Not just that, we've gained entry."

"Already?" He sounded genuinely shocked.

"Yep, there's more."

"What?" he gasped.

Me: "We've removed 2 vehicles full of stock."

"But they don't leave stock in vans overnight."

"Well, we didn't load them up and trust me. They are very full."

"Oh." He seemed quiet.

Me: "Shall we stop for the night? "

"If you want to…… But if you can do any more please let me know."

We removed 6 more vans… All full of boxes that we did not open.

My buddy cheekily walked up to the guard in the hut, who was suddenly on alert from being approached at this time of night – it obviously didn't happen often. And we gave the security guard an envelope addressed to the head of security, with all of the van keys in it.

Time to fire the guard?

Here's the thing. The guard allowed us to steal 8 vans. He was on security, and we broke in and stole a lot. But there were a lot of things that could have been done to prevent us from taking the vans:

- That security guard should not have been working on his own.
- If there had been a heater in the hut, he probably wouldn't have needed to take a walk every half an hour.
- If the door had been closed properly, we wouldn't have got into the building without setting off the alarm. Apparently, the door gets left open to give access to the smokers' area. The staff take the shortcut because they don't get time to go through the security doors, walk around to the designated area and smoke.
- If the key locker hadn't been in such a blatant place, we wouldn't have found it so quickly.
- Finally, if the key locker didn't have the key in the lock of the box, we wouldn't have been able to open it quite so easily!

Any one of these things COULD have stopped us.

But no one had done them.

And we got in WITHOUT breaking anything.

So many times, the jobs that I work on have very easy ways to fix any issues, but because we start having the "It won't happen" attitude, those issues don't get sorted. Just imagine the look on the employees face when they first start to notice something is wrong.

Would it have been the logistics manager who walked past where those vans should have been?

Maybe it was the first driver to notice the key missing for the van he had been given that day?

Either way, we probably could have been out of the country by the time they noticed. I was later told that we had taken vans with goods worth over half a million pounds.

Next time I might just take the vans!

USB stick

If you're using a desktop machine of any kind or if you have a laptop you will know the USB sticks can be very valuable, they can be there like a portable folder that you can just throw information onto. Did you know that they can also carry programs and when pushed into computer they can make the program run on the computer?

This means they're great way of stealing information off of your machine and getting it out of the building. You could have the best security system in the world, but if you've got one disgruntled employee or if you've got one person who gets physical access to your building, they can plug the USB stick into an open computer and download or plant whatever data or nefarious bit of software they want to. Earlier I was talking about key logging programs – using a USB stick you can automatically install one of these and you could send me all of that information without me having to go near your computer ever again.

Either of these types of attack can be very damaging to any company, no matter how large or how small, and it can bring them down.

How we can we fix this potential issue? It's actually quite easy! All you need to do is put USB locks into any USB port and it stops anyone from being able to gain physical access to that USB port. Do you even need USB ports in your machines? Perhaps your IT team just need to take them out! It is certainly not to be overlooked.

The Four Pillars

There are four main pillars to protecting your business: strategy, policy, education and testing.

Strategy

The reality is that even having read this book, it's a huge undertaking to start making your business secure. From my experience, most companies have only ever paid security lip service. Where do you go from here? Well as a starting point, use the checklist, it will likely highlight some basic things that you can do to get things sorted. But ongoing, you need strategies in place. Those strategies need to be clearly defined and budgeted for. It is impossible to do everything in one go, so you need to understand what actions need to be taken and the order of priority.

It is important to note here that those big figures of the fines should really be considered as part of this strategy. When we say that you need to define budgets and priorities, this is not an excuse to put a small nominal sum and have a plan that stretches off into the distance.

The other three pillars should be clearly defined as part of the strategy.

Policy

The style and size of your business will determine how heavily reliant on processes your company is. Having clear policies and processes in place, so that everyone knows what to do for different threats, is an absolute must. If a phishing email is received, do the staff know how to report it? What are the rules for letting people through reception? Are there rules on passwords?

If you are not clear on the communication of the policies and procedures, then you will get mistakes and potential breaches.

Education

Teaching people about the dangers is a massive part of protecting your business. If you are only learning about some of the dangers through reading this book, then your staff are probably completely unaware. Try to make sure that you provide information, regular updates and training. They should also have training on the policies to make sure they understand how to follow them. Of course, buying a load of copies of this book for them to read won't hurt!

I do a lot of training for large organisations who have taken a stance of duty of care to their staff, helping to educate them on the dangers and threats.

Testing

How do you know if you have weak points? What are the weakest parts of your system?

Without proper testing, you will not know how you will be attacked. Hiring someone to test your security will help you to understand the weakest links and give you direction with your strategy planning.

Full Circle

As you can see, we have ended up with strategy planning. This is because you should cycle these pillars, constantly updating your security strategy with the latest information, updating your policies, training your staff and testing the system.

Chapter 8
At The Shops

There are some scams that feature specifically in shops, bars and restaurants. The rules here are the same as before, staff need to be aware and vigilant, and owners need to make sure that they and their staff are protected. But because it almost effects both staff and owners at the same time and is specifically for this type of establishment, we thought we would separate it out from what feels rather more corporate. Firstly, one that has hit a lot of people that Jesse and I know.

Changing up some money...

This scam is despicable because it doesn't gain a great deal of cash for a scammer, but it is enough to affect the victim. It makes you feel extremely belittled and embarrassed, but the reality is it happens a lot because it is both easy to do and preys on the nature of being a customer serving person. To be honest this has gotten harder to pull off in the UK since we got rid of £1 notes BUT IT IS STILL POSSIBLE. It is however still very easy to do with $1 bills – so if you are in the U.S. please listen a bit closer...

A person comes into your shop and asks if they can change 10 single dollar bills into a $10 dollar note – knowing this is good for shops to have change in their till. You say yes and proceed to help them.

They hold out 10 single dollar bills which they have separated from a few 10-dollar notes that they also have. You hand them the $10 dollar note. They hand you the singles.

You notice there are only 9 there and say that they forgot one! After a quick apology, another bill is handed over.

"Actually a $20 would be much better If I give you one of the 10-dollar bills as well could you make it a $20 bill instead?"

You see no problem with this and agree, you still have the 10 singles, and you give them a $20 in return for a ten.

The only time you notice anything wrong is when you cash up at the end of the night and you're $10 down in the till.

What actually happened?

It's so simple and so deceptive all at the same time which is possibly why criminals love this scam!

When he asked for a $20 instead, he didn't actually give you $10 on top, he just handed you the one that was from your till in the first place!

You now have the 10 singles they gave you, a 10-dollar bill FROM YOU and you give them a 20-dollar bill for it!

I know this one can really annoy people who don't like maths, but if you ever want a full-on demonstration of it please give us a shout! The key here is to never feel rushed – you are better off laying the cash out to work out what they have given you and what you have given them.

Phone call to your boss.

A delivery driver comes into your office or your shop or your place of work. They've got a delivery for your boss, but it can be signed for by anyone. The snag is that there is a delivery charge for it. It has an outstanding amount of say £15 or £25; it's not a massive amount but it's just enough for you to say sorry I can't do that.

Your boss isn't actually in the office at the moment which seems a bit strange why would he arrange a delivery that would have to be paid for. The driver asks you if you could give your boss a call. You see no problem with this, so you call and explain that there's a delivery driver here with a product or something that he's ordered and you've got a pay for it. The driver then says "Can I talk to him?", so you hand over the phone.

You listen in on the conversation and everything seems to go okay. While you're listening, it's pointed out that the person at the shop can just take the £25 out of the till pay for it, keep a receipt and it will be dealt with tomorrow. Your boss comes in the next day and sees his delivery.

"What happened about the payment?"

"I did exactly what you said and paid for it out of the till."

"I never agreed to that!"

What actually happened is when you handed the phone over to the delivery driver your boss told them not to leave the thing and that they were not going to pay for anything that they didn't know about. It should be taken back to the depot. The driver nodded and agreed with them waited for your boss to hang up the phone and then pretended the conversation was carrying on.

They then went through a script that they had in their head which made it look like the boss has said take £25 out of the till and pay them directly. The till is now down £25 you have a delivery which is probably a cardboard box with a brick in it and the driver has scammed you out of some money. What's worse is that you thought you were helping your boss when you actually helped them get scammed. The moral of this story is always hear it from the horse's mouth!

How I could have robbed a jewellery store with a piece of paper

I work with a team of people and every so often one of them will give me an idea for a piece I could write about, a blog, an email, an article etc. and this one comes due to a chat with Matthew – his words were along the lines of "Paul you need to do a piece titled How I robbed a jewellery store with a piece of paper" Now, I have to be very careful with a lot of the things I'm currently working on and there are contracts I've signed that limit me from telling specific stories etc so I came back with a quick "No" to him.

This is now titled "How I could have robbed a jewellery store with a piece of paper"

And this story is complete fantasy.

I didn't do this.

I was approached by a very nice gent who owned a few retail outlets. Let's say they sell bread. He was worried that his store managers were getting a bit too laid back with security because they had never had a significant theft from their stores.

He asked me how much dough I thought I could steal without them noticing until I was very far away from the store.

Dough... Yeah, I went there!

Anyway, I had a long hard look at the problem, worked out what I wanted to do, and it was scarily easy.

A buddy and I found out where one of the store assistants went for a drink. We turned up at that establishment and did some entertaining for the crowds, when we got to this young lady, we did some hypnosis. I'm not going to get into the massive chat about if hypnosis is real or not right now let's just "pretend" that it is.

While entertaining her and her friends we placed a lovely suggestion in her head. The next time she saw me she would believe that my blank paper was in fact money. Two days later I walk into the store while she's working. I browse the assortment of pastry-based products and pick a few things out. One piece looked particularly lovely on my wrist...

I paid this lovely lady with blank paper.

She even handed me my change...

If I had written this book at the time of stealing that breadstick, I probably wouldn't have put it in the book – what benefit to you is it? The difference is that nowadays security camera systems are much clearer and much more affordable. We even have them in our homes and in our doorbells these days. In fact, for not that much money I can get a cloud enabled security camera baby monitor which would be better than most CCTV prior to about 10 years ago.

I know the reality is that someone hypnotising members of staff is not a risk most business owners are going to react to! But it's impossible to stop all criminal activity, nothing is ever fool proof. At least with a security camera you stand a chance of catching the criminal, you can show it to your insurance company, and you can also look out for potential weaknesses in security.

Chapter 9
Preying On Fear

Working alongside Jesse has taught me a few things, one of which is that people make decisions based on our emotions, rather than using our logic. In fact, we will often skew our logic to reinforce the way that we feel about something.

Many people tell me that fear stands for False Evidence Appearing Real. But I've never liked that one.

The Oxford Dictionary says it better - that the word fear is:

"an unpleasant emotion caused by the threat of danger, pain, or harm."

That sounds a bit more like what Jesse said. Scammers use this emotion as a way to control us. They want us in that horrendous space where everything feels uneasy, making us feel that moment of fight or flight.

They will use the fact that we're worried about losing our money. We're worried about being in trouble with the law. We fear for other people's safety. We are frightened for our own safety. We are frightened of upsetting a client. We worry about making the boss angry.

All this fear is fantastic for a scammer. It makes you susceptible to suggestions of ways to get away from the cause of fear. We don't like to feel frightened for long periods of time, we want to reduce the stress. All of this leads to snap decisions and being led in the wrong direction!

What can we do to reduce fear?

We can learn, we can adapt, we can change, and we can grow.
There will always be something to fear, but the fact is that we can control that fear. We can control our securities and our insecurities. We can create defences that will make us look unbreakable and with the best will in the world the people that try to break us will choose to look the other way. Remember:

"I don't need to outrun the bear.... I just need to outrun you........"

Can you even control that fear?

Think about it this way. There are some people who could be right in the middle of a massive car crash, but they're so cool and calm it's ridiculous. Think of the ambulance crew that knows they're going into someone else's version of hell, but they need to be able to assess everything and make the calls that could save people's lives.

If you ever start to feel fear taking over, I want YOU to be in full control of IT. Not the other way round.

So here we go – Paul's take on dealing with fear.

1 Stop. Take a breath

Just this pause alone will get your brain in to gear. Taking just a moment of time to think rationally will help in any stressful situation.

2 Feel

Notice what you are going through and recognise it. Remind yourself that you are only human and anyone in this situation would start having these feelings.

3 Face it

You've realised they're trying to scam you. Assess the situation. How much danger are you REALLY in? How much control do you have?

4 What's the worst?

Honestly, what's the worst thing that can happen? Now take realistic steps back from it and work a way towards the best that can happen.

5 Check the evidence

What are they telling you? Can you prove they are wrong? Do you need to get someone else involved?

6 Take emotion out of it

To the scammer this is just a business transaction – nothing more, nothing less. Can you look at it in the same way?

7 Talk about it

As soon as you can. Tell other people what happened, how they tried to scam you, how you felt, what you did, how you felt afterwards. The more you talk about it the less it will make you feel.

8 Reward yourself

You've done this, you got through it. Give yourself a cheeky reward for dealing with these people!

Fear should be recognised as our own body giving us a warning that something just isn't right. It can be used, and it can be tamed. Listen to it, feel it and then use it to your advantage.

Time for some Military Training

The military trains people to deal with stressful situations – officers need to command soldiers and take control of stressful situations. As part of this, they often play the scene from Saving Private Ryan where they arrive on Omaha beach. Tom Hanks' character freezes with fear, looking at the situation around him. But then he takes a quiet moment to take a deep breath, sort out the emotions and deal with the task in hand.

Hopefully you will never have to deal with such a horrific situation, but that level of stress and fear is what the scammer is trying to push on you. If you can take that moment, you will feel clear and capable to handle the situation. As you take that moment, the scammer will try to push harder, to try and force you to feel pressured again. Recognising that is when you have got them – you know they are a scammer and you know that you aren't going to play their game.

Chapter 10
You got scammed...

Are you going to deny it? After all we have been through together, are you really going to say it didn't happen? I started this book with talking about all of the emotions you feel when you have been scammed – and now is the time you are feeling them. Just as long as you do not live in denial, things will be ok.

There are two main reasons that I don't like to ignore scams. The first is, you may be surprised to hear, that you can often do something about it. The second is, we need to talk about it to raise awareness.

Do Something About It

It's a very difficult thing to do, but once you have been scammed, it is important to try and put your feelings and emotions to one side. You need to deal with this – and you know that the only emotion that the scammer is feeling is smug. Let's put your game face on and wipe that look off of the scammer.

We always used to start with alerting the authorities, which for some of the more conventional scams is still your best bet. But actually the number of cyber scams that are happening are increasing at such a high rate that it is often hard to speak to the right person, or to get useful and timely advice from the right people because they are so inundated. These days there are some absolute superheroes that can help you if you are victims of a cybercrime – The Cyber Helpline.

www.thecyberhelpline.com

The Cyber Helpline provide free, expert advice for victims of cybercrime. If you have been scammed, or think you have been hacked, they are the people to get advice from.

Of course, if your bank account has been hacked, it is worth contacting your bank to let them know there is a situation, but if you can get some quick advice from The Cyber Helpline then you will know that you are not going to miss anything.

There are a wide range of different scams and ways of getting hacked, so it would be impossible for me to comment on dealing with all of them. That said, I can advise that the quicker you act the more likely you are to get a positive outcome – so get going.

Whether or not it is a positive outcome, the next step is to protect yourself. Follow the advice, change your passwords (ideally with a password tool). No-one is 100% safe, so if you have been scammed, acknowledge it, and learn from the experience.

What should I do if I've been a victim of a phone scam?

Scammers are constantly finding new ways to trick people and phone scams are changing all the time. If you've been the victim of a scam don't be embarrassed to report it. It can happen to anyone.

Report the scam to the police and also contact Action Fraud. The information you give to Action Fraud can help track down the scammer.

No More Taboo

This is often the hardest part of being scammed - talking about it. Let people know that there is a risk. This is the point of this book – the more people know, the more they can protect themselves, and the harder it is for scammers.

You personally may not have the reach to help a lot of people – but people like me will always welcome your story. If I can share it with a lot of people, either telling it as your story, or by keeping you anonymous, we can help as many people as possible. The issue is the taboo that is brought around by it – people are worried by the bad press associated with scams and being hacked – no one likes to show weakness. However, with the fact that an estimated 51% of businesses experienced "denial of service" attacks in 2018, this is something that a lot of people are dealing with.

Is It Really Worth It?

The thing that stops a lot of people doing anything is that they think there is an amount that isn't worth the effort. Or alternatively, they think that whatever has been hacked is unimportant.

It takes 280 days average time to identify and contain a breach in security. For individuals it can take years; I have helped people deal with small amounts of Direct Debit payments going out every month for 5 years – and when you add that up, it's a number worth taking seriously.

I have already discussed the issue with malware that sees everything that is going on in your computer. There is no such thing as a little hack. It means you are at risk. The simple answer is yes, it is always worth investigating and dealing with a scam.

Chapter 11
Strong. Confident. Wary.

Jesse and I talk about a lot of things. Sometimes they relate to MentalTheft and how it's all going. Sometimes we talk about "Pinky and the Brain". Some days are more productive than others! On this occasion we were talking about what MentalTheft is and why the business exists; why does MentalTheft need to be around? This led on to the question: what do we want people to get out of us and our journey?

In fact, this book is a journey. Apart from scaring you to death, and giving some insight and bits of advice, what will your overall take be on MentalTheft? Not just as a book, but as an idea. A statement came out of this conversation that kind of hit me square between the eyes.

Strong. Confident. Wary.

It says everything we need you to feel.

It explains that we want people to ditch the fear of the world. We want you to feel the strength of making the right choices, making sure your backside is covered as well as it can be. To walk confidently through all your transactions, online or offline. All of this whilst listening to that little voice in your head when it says, "is that person trying to see your PIN?"

If we can do all of these things, we can get rid of the 99 out of 100 ways that a scammer will attack you. The stronger you look the more they will want to look elsewhere. Another statement that I use all the time, if you have ever seen me speak in real life, you'll already know it:

Trust but verify.
It's a MASSIVE statement, while remaining so simple.

You can trust anyone that you talk to. And if they're good people they will have no issue with you verifying their information.

If they are a scammer, they will hate the idea and they'll try to put more pressure onto you to make the quick decision in their favour.

It also struck us that this phrase should even be used on yourself.

Don't trust your gut
If we told you that we were going to fling you against a strap with the force of a hundred hammers, you will probably say "no thanks, that will chop me in half". We know that this is the reality of that situation. But we also know that with stretchy material, a specialist lever system, and most importantly an awful lot of testing, we are happy that this strap, otherwise known as a seatbelt, is likely to save your life.

The problem is that with a lot of the MentalTheft situations that we have described, especially the ones pertaining to cyber security, you don't have the knowledge to understand what is good and bad. I have bleated on about password protectors, but can you really trust them? Am I just lying to you? In the story by Sheryl, she talked about how the idea of a password checker felt almost counter intuitive. But she asked people who she trusted, she asked people who were in the know. I encourage you to look up all of my advice. Don't trust me – I cheat for a living!! I like to think I'm more of a loveable rogue – like Robin Hood, I am technically on your side.

But remember:

Trust but verify.

Only through learning and knowledge can you know what risks are out there, and how best to deal with them. The strength and sense of empowerment once you realise that you know how to protect yourself. The fact that you are ready for anything. This is the MentalTheft martial art.

Strong. Confident. Wary.

Chapter 12
Checklists

So, to feeling strong, confident and wary – and what better way to get your ducks in a row? Well, it all feels a little bit much doesn't it? I mean, we are so many chapters in, where do we start with all of this? How do we cover all of that off? Well, here is where this book turns into more of an exercise book.

The following is a set of checklists, laid out with space to put notes and to tick off each area. If you see gaps, or need to do more work, that's fine, do some note writing. But be careful – I don't want to steal this book back off you and see your passwords or any sensitive information written down!

Computer checklist
Internet and computer

- ☐ USE A PASSWORD MANAGER!
- ☐ You may have heard that bit before somewhere, so here is something else... Set up two factor authentication on every account that you can.
- ☐ Set up child controls

DO NOT write down any of your passwords. So many people write them in a book and keep it in the top drawer of their desk... please don't be one of those people! If you do get robbed, how difficult do you think it is for someone to look though that stuff and access all of your accounts? They probably don't even need the computer they stole, as most of it will be online!

Notes

The Catfish checklist

- [ ] Are they on social media?
- [ ] Are they on other social media too?
- [ ] How many friends are they connected to?
- [ ] How many photos do they have?
- [ ] Are the photos close-up or only from a long distance?
- [ ] How many friends do they have?
- [ ] What is the quality of the photos like?
- [ ] Are they interacting with other people?
- [ ] Is it just you and them, or are you in a group?
- [ ] Have they asked you for money?

Notes

Home security checklist
Your boundaries

- [ ] Fences, walls and hedges: check for damage and gaps and repair as soon as possible. Prickly plants are a good deterrent and can also be used under vulnerable ground floor windows.
- [ ] A low boundary at the front of your property ensures good visibility from passers-by and your neighbours – the Home Office recommend shrubs are kept to a maximum height of 1 metre.
- [ ] Your boundary at the back of your property should be approximately 2 metres high. You can increase security by using anti-climb paint or "prickler" strip along the top of fences (with appropriate warning signage). Adding a trellis panel not only increases height but is too fragile to bear body weight, therefore increasing the risk to a burglar.
- [ ] Are side entrances secure? Replace any damaged or rusty hinges, hasps and padlocks.
- [ ] Good lighting is essential to deter a burglar – the police recommend the use of low-level dusk-till-dawn lighting. It is cheap to buy and uses less electricity than halogen lamps. Solar lighting can also help illuminate isolated areas
- [ ] Consider other warning devices to let you know someone has come onto your property, such as a gravel drive or a driveway alarm.

Notes

Doors

- ☐ Check the framework around your external doors (including patio and French doors). Frames should be securely fixed to the wall and in good condition.
- ☐ Check the thickness of doors: an external door should be a minimum of 44mm if you want to fit a mortised deadlock – if the door is too thin, then a surface mount lock should be fitted.
- ☐ Do you have any wooden panelled doors? Are they strong enough? Often panels are made of a thinner material, but these can be easily replaced with something more sturdy.
- ☐ Ideally front doors should be secured in two places – usually a mortised deadlock at a mid-point in the door with a Yale-type latch lock approximately 60-80cm above it. The more places a door is secured to the frame, the stronger it will be.
- ☐ Consider fitting a door viewer, a door chain or bar and even a letterbox cage or locking letterbox plate.
- ☐ Does your patio door have suitable frame locks or an anti-lift device? If not, most double-glazing companies can fit these for you. French doors should lock to each other as well as to the top and bottom of the door frame.

Notes

Windows

- [ ] Check the frames of your windows and repair any damage. Pay special attention to those that are vulnerable (ground floor, at the rear of the building, accessible by a flat roof).
- [ ] Modern UPVC windows now have locks fitted as standard – British Standard BS7950 – and can be fitted with additional window restrictors and sash jammers.
- [ ] Are the windowpanes made from laminated glass – this is glass that is extremely difficult to break. Don't confuse laminated glass with toughened glass, which is designed for safety.
- [ ] Don't forget to check garage windows, especially if the garage is attached to the home with an internal access door.
- [ ] Garage and shed windows can be obscured with frosted adhesive vinyl – if a burglar can't see in, it reduces the temptation to break in.
- [ ] Leaded glazing and wood/metal framed windows: these are not very secure unless you fit secondary laminated glazing, polycarbonate sheeting, or internal grilles.

Notes

Locks

- [ ] Locks are only as good as the screws and framework they are attached to – replace any damaged parts.
- [ ] The recommended type of mortise lock is a five-lever lock to British Standard BS3621 / EN12209 (most house insurance policies insist on this specification for the front door).
- [ ] If you've got a Yale-style latch lock, is it double locking (i.e., if you turn the key, does the block stay in place effectively making it a deadlock)? These are more secure, especially if the lock is near a glass panel in the door.
- [ ] Mortise bolts operate only from the inside and are suitable for French doors and sliding patio doors, and are best placed at the top and bottom of the door.

Notes

Outbuildings

- [ ] Give your locks and bolts a "health check" – replace any rusty items, ensure all padlocks and hasps bear the British Standard kite mark and are made of hardened steel.
- [ ] Don't forget the hinges on your doors – if a burglar can't breach the lock, they may attempt to unscrew the hinges. Use coach bolts, non-return screws or simply damage the screw head; you don't need to do every screw, just a couple on the hanging plate and a couple on the door plate.
- [ ] Remember to secure outbuilding windows – even the ones that don't open can be vulnerable. Consider obscuring the window with an opaque window film (the type used on bathroom windows) as this will reduce the temptation. Alternatively, fit a grille or a couple of bars across the inside of the window to reduce the window aperture.
- [ ] Consider using a battery-operated siren alarm in your garage or shed - they often cost less than £20 (in 2020) and are simple to install and use.
- [ ] Get into the good habit of putting everything away when you have finished with it. Your tools can be used against your house.

Notes

Property Marking

- [ ] Property marking cannot prevent your goods from being stolen but it is a very good deterrent as it is difficult to sell on stolen property that has been marked. It also allows the police to return recovered stolen goods to their rightful owner. Mark your property with your house/flat number and postcode.
- [ ] Use a UV pen or a chemical DNA marking solution to invisibly mark items such as mobile phones, audio-visual equipment, cameras, etc.
- [ ] Items you don't mind spoiling the look of something, such as garden equipment and power tools: security mark them by etching or scratching your postcode on to them.
- [ ] Don't forget to open an account with www.immobilise.com – this is a free national online asset register where you can record details of your property. If your property is lost or stolen, immobilise aids the police with their investigations and helps to disrupt the second-hand market.

Notes

Burglar alarms & domestic CCTV

- ☐ There are many types of alarm and CCTV systems, from wired and monitored systems at the top of the range down to battery-operated wire-free systems. Consider which is the most appropriate for your needs and how much you want to spend.
- ☐ Please bear in mind that, although wire-free systems are an effective deterrent, most insurance companies do not recognise these systems so will not acknowledge them on your policy specification.
- ☐ To find a reputable alarm and CCTV fitter, contact your local Trading Standards and ask about their "Approved Traders Scheme".

Notes

Business security checklist

First of all – go check the homeowner's checklist! Anything that is applicable there – DO IT! Secondly, this is not the most in-depth list ever. Please use common sense and take advice from an expert that could look at your business in depth!

Boundaries

- [ ] Gates, turnstiles etc. Ensure they are undamaged and check that they are actually locked when not in use
- [ ] Light it up! Burglars love the dark – Don't make it easy for them!
- [ ] Anti-Climb Measures
- [ ] Secure the perimeter

Notes

Good locks!

- [ ] Review and replace locks if needed
- [ ] Smart Access (Smart locks etc)
- [ ] Fit an alarm

Notes

Security guards
(You will know if your company can justify it or not!)

- ☐ Be Vigilant
- ☐ Do you have enough to cover all of the entrances?
- ☐ Are they stationery or do they need to be patrolling?
- ☐ Do you have a testing regime? Don't just assume they are doing a good job

---

Notes

Online and cyber security

- [ ] Do you have someone in charge of your IT?
- [ ] Is your IT person an IT expert?
- [ ] Are you GDPR compliant?
- [ ] Are you backing up your data?
- [ ] Do you have a Cyber Security Strategy?
- [ ] Do you have a comprehensive set of cyber security policies?
- [ ] Have you educated your staff about the risks?
- [ ] Do you have systems and policies on portable devices such a laptops, tablets and smart phones?

Notes

If you have said no to any of the above, you might consider contacting Aerice... www.aerice.com to help you with making your strategy, the easy way.

Chapter 13
Our Sponsors

This book was written with the help of a lot of people, both from the stories that I gratefully received, to the funding of the publishing of the book. We completed a very successful crowdfunding campaign, which I think was a mix of generosity from some lovely people and a general feeling that this book is needed.

I would like to say a massive thank you to those sponsors, and to the corporate sponsors that knew that MentalTheft was a crowd they wanted to be seen with, here is an extra thank you!

Please take the time to see how some truly fantastic businesses can help you personally and your company.

Aerice

When it comes to Cyber Security, you are probably feeling a bit overwhelmed and out of control. Getting a strategy in place that is practical for your operations and your budget seems impossible and you probably don't even know where to start.

Aerice are an unusual business, breaking the mould of what consultancy really is. With specialist capability in cyber security and GDPR, amongst many other things, Aerice will work to your company's needs to not only build a strategy, but also bring together whatever is necessary to implement that strategy.

With a philosophy of "getting things done" Aerice will work with you to complete projects in a practical time frame, rather leaving you with a strategy that is out of date before it is live.

Having come together with this unusual philosophy, their core beliefs and way of working means that they can successfully deliver to SMEs and large global and government organisations alike. They believe that consultancy doesn't have to cost the earth or involve endless consultancy cycles. Whether you require half a day review or a large implementation schedule, consisting of many facets, then they are always happy to help.

Taking an outcomes-based approach to all of their engagements, the Aerice team defines their exit strategy ahead of each engagement. They will work with you to confirm the outcomes you are seeking to achieve and to understand any constraints you may have, and ensure the project is designed and structured to deliver exactly what you require from it. This enables them to exit at the right point, ensuring a strong focus on delivering results as swiftly as possible and ensuring our clients are left feeling they have achieved great value for money.

Aerice strongly believe clients should be in control of their budgets throughout and never over scope or overcomplicate engagements to increase your consultancy spend.

aerice.com

Biscoes Law

As one of Hampshire's leading, full-service law firms, Biscoes advise businesses, organisations and individuals on all of their legal needs in Hampshire and the Isle of Wight. Because they're driven by your needs, not their own, they work hard to understand your requirements. The Biscoes people are flexible, proactive problem solvers, who use law as a tool to provide innovative and tailored solutions that deliver a better outcome for you, or for your business.

Clarity of costs is key to the service that Biscoes provide. Projects are defined by the work that will and will not be covered, how costs are calculated and any assumptions that have been made to come up with the cost estimate. This helps them to mitigate surprises and keep you in control of the budget.

Working on both personal and business law, the quality of the service provided by Biscoes is exceptional, as their long list of customer recommendations are testament to.

www.biscoes-law.co.uk/

Genio Accountants

Southampton based accountancy firm Genio Accountants have decades of combined experience. Their work has been both as financial personnel in business, as well as practice accountancy, which allows them to work with small local businesses with an understanding of the issues that they face.

As Xero Accounting gold accredited partners, and experts in Sage, Genio help businesses with using the right software for their company, whilst providing setup and development as necessary to make the tools work from you.

Available for appointments booked outside of standard office hours, the team pride themselves on both the quality of the service and their level of customer care. If you are looking for an accountancy firm to help you manage your business finances, why not contact Genio Accountants?

www.genio-accountants.co.uk

Family Wise

Family Wise Ltd are experts in finding people, whether it is for probate and intestacy research ('Heir Hunting'), locating missing relatives, private investigation or professional family history research around the world. They provide exceptional services whether you are interested in your family history or are trying to trace a living next-of-kin.

family-wise.co.uk

Step By Step Listening

Offering personal and business coaching, Step by Step Listening help people to listen better to help build relationships. Well known for their work with managing your critic, Sheryl leads the way in helping you to do more of what you love and ditch the critic that says that you can't. Working without judgement, they offer a range of services to help you experience the power of clarity.

www.stepbysteplistening.com

Fresh Security

Fresh Security offer a subscription-based service to monitor the email addresses of your whole business, highlighting potential risks and helping you keep out hackers. By monitoring high risk email addresses across the dark web, Fresh Security looks for data such as passwords associated with your business email accounts to allow you to protect yourself and your staff against scammers.

www.mentaltheft.co.uk/email-security

Forest Edge Solicitors

Forest Edge Solicitors are a Ringwood based solicitors' firm, providing a local service with an aim to being "here when you need us". Providing high levels of customer care, the team are responsive and friendly, whether you need personal or business solicitor services. Available for out of hours appointments, meetings can be in person, phone or via video call.

www.forestedgesolicitors.co.uk

JLawrence Photography

Experienced and friendly new forest-based photographer, perfect for couples who don't like having their picture taken but want beautiful wedding photographs.

Do you hate having your photo taken?

It's no surprise if you do – people in the UK, especially women, have one of the lowest levels of positive body image in the world. Even if you are a selfie queen, you probably hate people taking your photo. Here's the conundrum:

You still want stunning photographs of you on your wedding day!

One of the main reasons that people love to have Jesse as their photographer is that he makes people feel comfortable and able to be natural. In this way, he can capture you and your partner in a natural beauty like you have never seen before.

Jesse is extremely passionate about helping couples enjoy their wedding day. He has a relaxed style, but works extremely hard, making sure that you feel comfortable on the most important day of your life, whilst getting images that make you smile and glow.

> *"Jesse did the photos of our wedding back in july this year and was so professional but approachable at the same time. Like most people we're not the most comfortable with having our photos taken and wanted to make sure we spent most of the day with our friends and family rather than posing endlessly. With the help of jesse we managed to have this whilst still getting loads of amazing and natural photos too. Would recommend to anyone getting married or in need of a photographer for any other reason as he's easy to talk to and really understands what you want from your day."*

Katrina, Bride, The New Forest

www.jlawrence-photography.co.uk/

Chapter 14
Hiring Paul Newton

Paul has worked across many industries and understands both business and people. Having become well known as one of the country's top magicians, he is often seen at stage shows, events and weddings. However, since the birth of MentalTheft, Paul's "other life" of dealing with scammers and crime has come to the forefront of his life. It is fair to say that however you know Paul, his hard work, friendly yet frank nature and love of hugs has made him a well-known character!

Hire MentalTheft

Available for public speaking, either as a trainer for business events, or at corporate events.

If you are hosting a corporate event and need a public speaker, why not hire me to steal your sh1t? As a magician and MentalTheft expert, I will wow your audience with incredible magic, such as stealing PINs, placing ideas and making people believe things that didn't happen. But it's not just a magic show, I talk about the real issues behind theft of the mind - such as being able to protect yourselves against hackers and thieves.

Did I seriously just say Sh1t?

Sure, it's hard hitting, people take notice. But there's more to it than that. In the early days of computing people used passwords such as God, but these days a lot of people use swearwords - common passwords are the easiest to crack. People also often change letters for numbers that look similar, thinking that these are more difficult to hack. They are not! Although this is a provocative title to my talks, it really does have a strong foundation in what I do.

As well as public speaking, Paul is available for training and consultancy.

www.mentaltheft.co.uk

Hire Paul Newton Magic

Whether it is for a wedding, charity event, or party, Paul is available to provide premium quality close-up and table magic.

Whether you are trying to make your wedding extra special, or wanting to make your charity fundraiser or party the most talked about event of the year, Paul will keep your guests entertained. Breaking the magician stereotype of weird and awkward, he is friendly and personable, making your guests feel relaxed so that they have a great time whilst being wowed.

It is not just events, however. Having performed, in headline acts at prestigious venues such as the Bournemouth International Centre (BIC), as well as at business events for large corporations such as O2, Paul is well versed in stage show magic to entertain a large audience.

Exhibition Management

Set up your exhibition workflow to maximise the number of quality leads that you receive with more than just entertainment at your stand. Draw prospects to your stand with close up magic tricks and subtle base level qualification that will not only ensure that your salespeople only talk to quality leads, but the introduction also improves follow-up and conversion rates.

www.paul-newton.co.uk

Newton's Nuggets

Known for his popular show, Newton's Nuggets, available via YouTube or Podcasts, these interviews have brought together Paul's world of entertainment and MentalTheft!

With only two basic rules, the show has a regular and ever growing following:
1. Guests must be interesting!
2. Guests must provide one nugget of useful information or advice

From film star, stuntman and magician Matthew Stirling, to cyber security expert Graeme McGowan, this weekly show has become bigger than Paul could ever have imagined!

#newtonsnuggets